52 Weeks of Sales Success

America's #1 Salesman Shows You How to Send Sales Soaring!

Second Edition

Ralph R. Roberts
with Joe Kraynak

WILEY

John Wiley & Sons, Inc.

Published by John Wiley & Sons, Inc., Hoboken, New Jersey.
Published simultaneously in Canada.

For general information on our other products and services or for technical support, please contact our Customer Care Department within the United States at (800) 762-2974, outside the United States at (317) 572-3993 or fax (317) 572-4002.

Wiley also publishes its books in a variety of electronic formats. Some content that appears in print may not be available in electronic books. For more information about Wiley products, visit our web site at www.wiley.com.

Library of Congress Cataloging-in-Publication Data:

Roberts, Ralph R., 1958–
    52 weeks of sales success: America's #1 salesman shows you how to send sales soaring! / Ralph Roberts, with Joe Kraynak.—2nd ed.
        p. cm.
    Includes index.
    ISBN 978-0-470-39350-5 (pbk.)
1. Selling.   I. Kraynak, Joe.   II. Title.
HF5438.25.R583 2009
658.85—dc22

                                                                    2008032164

Printed in the United States of America.

10 9 8 7 6 5 4 3 2 1

Contents

Preface

B y most people's standards, I am highly successful. What success means to me, however, encompasses much more than professional success. It conveys a sense of balance. After all, if you are successful in sales at the expense of your health, your relationships, or your soul, what have you really achieved?

In this book, I present 52 lessons that I gleaned from my 30-year career in sales. Most of these lessons encourage you and show you how to achieve not only what I consider sales success but also how to lead a successful life. By putting these lessons into practice, you will be able to sell more and earn more while spending less time and effort doing it. You will be able to focus on what you do best—selling and serving your customers—and outsource the rest to people who are better equipped to play a supporting role. You will have more time to pursue your dreams, spend quality time with your significant others, and contribute to your community. Your life will become more rewarding and fulfilling.

I have written other books on the art of selling, including *Advanced Selling For Dummies* and *Walk Like a Giant, Sell Like a Madman*. During the writing of this book, I was also co-authoring *Cross-Cultural Selling For Dummies* with my friend and colleague cross-cultural selling specialist Michael Soon Lee. I believe that all of these books are excellent resources on the how-to of selling. I believe that *52 Weeks of Sales Success* is special, however, because it steps you through the process over the course of a year, providing bite-sized bits of wisdom that you can implement over time rather than getting overwhelmed by trying to do everything at once.

I practice these lessons myself, and during the time when my career was focused on selling homes, the strategies I describe in this book helped me boost sales from a previously unheard of 300 homes a year to an incredible 600 homes per year—almost a hundred times what an average Realtor does each 12 months. I quote these figures not to boast (after all, a lot of talented and dedicated people helped me achieve that mark), but to prove that the strategies I developed and present in this book really work.

This book is a product of my Monday morning meetings with my staff. During these meetings, I have always had the goal of teaching my sales staff a new strategy or technique. I figured if I could teach them one valuable lesson per week, by the end of the year, they would have all the knowledge and skills required to become top producers in our very competitive marketplace.

In essence, this book is the recorded version of a yearlong series of seminars that I conducted for my staff. Just as I took one important topic per week for them, I've decided to organize this book around a one-idea-a-week-for-52-weeks principle. You can read the book that way—one chapter per week—or you can read it all in one sitting and dip back into it when you need a refresher course. Or you can skip around to the topics that seem especially relevant to you. I've tried to make this book as flexible and as useful for you as I would want such a book to be for me and my staff.

Just as I introduced my staff to some of the nation's top salespeople, I'll let you meet some of them in these pages, too. For example, we'll be meeting Stephen Hopson, a remarkable young man who has won every sales award for stockbrokers that Merrill Lynch can give. And Patty Klein, a super travel agent here in Metro Detroit. And Jonathan Dwoskin, who taught me how to transfer basic sales techniques to the world of the Internet. And many, many more.

It's my goal to help all my readers realize that they, too, can be not only good salespeople, but great ones—true superstars. Sometimes people hear me speak and think that I must possess some magic elixir of success, or that I'm unnaturally talented. Neither is true. I started out in sales like many of you—a green 18-year-old kid with no college who had lots of dreams but not a clue how to make them come true. Thanks to some wonderful mentors and a lot of hard work, I've accomplished every one of my early dreams. Now I'm working on a whole set of new dreams—like changing the world one million people at a time. I know I'll get there someday, and this book will help.

If you take one lesson away from this book, it should be this: Your dreams can become reality. Don't be intimidated; don't be discouraged. We all have bad days, but success is just a matter of following the step-by-step path of progress that others have already laid out for you. I truly expect that this book will teach you a lesson a week to help you come up to me and say, "Thanks Ralph, your book helped make me a superstar just like you!"

Acknowledgments

The authors would like to thank our agent, Neil Salkind of Studio B (www.studiob.com), and our editor at John Wiley & Sons, Shannon Vargo, for breathing new life into one of Ralph's first and most successful books. Thanks also to Lois Maljak, Ralph's second in command, without whom this project would not have been possible. Special thanks to Ralph's wife (and girlfriend), Kathleen Roberts, who read and critiqued the entire manuscript and added her own personal touch. Thanks also to Ralph's team of dedicated and talented professionals who work side-by-side with Ralph in the trenches every day:

- Sue Bernier
- Lisa Doroh
- Paul Doroh
- Sarah Hodges
- Michele Milam
- Ismeta Preldzic
- Jessica Ruddle
- Jeannie Sample
- Steve Sample
- Joy Santiago
- Frank Sattler
- John Selby
- Michele Selby
- Lauren Wroblewski or McDowell or McDowellski or Wroblewski-McDowell (she can't decide since she just recently got married)

Thanks to the team at Wiley, including Jessica Langan-Peck and Linda Indig, for transforming a high-quality manuscript into an exceptional finished product and tying up any loose ends.

Numerous salespeople and other inspirational souls generously shared their ideas and stories with us (and ultimately with you, the reader). You will meet many of these individuals as you take the 52-week journey that is this book.

We would also like to thank the numerous salespeople who shared their ideas about their profession, reviewed specific chapters, and inspired some of the content. This book would be poorer without their help. Among those we want to thank specifically are the following:

- Mikal Belicove is a seasoned freelance writer, ghost blogger, and new media corporate communications consultant who's hotwired to the Internet and the Internet community. Mikal contributed his expertise to the chapters on corporate blogging and social media marketing. For more about Mikal, visit his blog at www.belicove.com.

- John Featherston, president and CEO of RISMedia (www.rismedia.com), was instrumental in the creation of Week 47, "Build Your Own Sales Team." John is an expert on building power teams for the real estate industry and publishes the monthly *Power Team Report* for RISMedia. Look for John's book, co-authored with Ralph R. Roberts, *Power Teams: The Complete Guide to Building and Managing a Winning Real Estate Agent Team.*

- Michael Soon Lee, MBA, is a diversity expert who speaks around the world on selling to multicultural customers. Michael's insights on multicultural marketing and cross-cultural selling inspired some of what we include in Week 45, "Expand into Multicultural Markets." Look for his book, co-authored with Ralph R. Roberts and Joe Kraynak, *Cross-Cultural Selling For Dummies.* To find out more about Michael and his multicultural approach, visit his web site at www.EthnoConnect.com.

- Terry Wisner, "The Life Saver Dude," created the Personal Partnering Process™ to help people become more successful both personally and professionally. He also inspired Week 33, "Team

Up with a Personal Partner." To learn how to bring clarity, focus, and accountability into your life, visit Terry's web site at www.TheLifeSaverDude.com or www.p2s.us.

- Terry Brock is a professional speaker and a columnist for business journals around the United States. He writes about technology, marketing, and the Internet in his weekly column, *Succeeding Today*. Terry's insights on R-commerce (relationship commerce) inspired Week 36, "Nurture Relationships." For more about Terry and what he has to offer, visit www.terrybrock.com.

WEEK 1

START NOW

Whenever I coach or mentor a salesperson following my 52 Weeks of Sales Success approach, I'm invariably asked, "So, when do we get started?" And I invariably answer, "Now."

Prior to implementing any self-improvement program—weight loss, smoking cessation, whatever—many people give themselves a grace period to indulge their cravings. They'll start dieting after Thanksgiving, for example, or stop smoking on Monday.

For some people, this approach might work, but for many people, when that date finally arrives, they simply bump out the date. They still have half a box of candy or a few cigarettes left that they don't want to waste, so they put it off until they've depleted their supply. In the meantime, they buy some more candy or cigarettes, and end up never getting around to following up on their good intentions.

If you are serious about boosting sales and profits, start making changes today, right now. As soon as you have a plan in place, start working the plan immediately. Why wait? Seize the opportunity now!

DO THE HARDEST THING FIRST

What keeps most people from getting started at the beginning of the day is that they wake up facing a difficult or distasteful task that they do not even want to think about. Ironically, this becomes all they think about, and then they look for any distraction they can think of to avoid performing that task.

To start your day right, tackle the task you find most difficult or unpleasant first. If you hate making phone calls, do it early in the morning rather than waiting until the end of the day. If you plan on having a difficult encounter with a colleague or one of your assistants, deal with it immediately rather than letting it ruin your entire day. Get it out of the way, so you can start to look forward to what you truly love about your work and to your dollar-productive activities—tasks that carry the promise of generating revenue.

If "Do the Hardest Thing First" doesn't quite work for you, consider some variations on this approach. The key is to become productive as early as possible in the day. Here are some other suggestions for starting your day off right:

- *Take a step-by-step approach.* Jot down a list of everything you need to get done today and prioritize items on the list.
- *Perform the most profitable tasks first.* Focus on dollar-productive (revenue-generating) tasks first.
- *Perform the easiest tasks first.* If tackling the most difficult task is just too overwhelming, consider dealing with something easy to work up some momentum.
- *Perform the most obvious tasks first.* If a task obviously needs to be accomplished before you can perform other tasks, tackle the obvious task first.

I generally tackle the most difficult tasks first. I call the people I don't want to talk to, address any problems that cross my desk, and immediately tend to the task I am most strongly inclined to avoid. Then, I focus on the most profitable (dollar-productive or revenue-generating) activities. I learned about dollar-productive activities from the "Condo King," Allen Domb, while shadowing him. If I have any time left near the end of the day, I deal with the remaining items on my list in their order of importance.

TELL EVERYONE YOU KNOW WHAT YOU DO

If you have just launched your career in sales, the very first step you need to take to be successful is to tell everyone you know about your job, and I mean everybody—friends, family members, neighbors, acquaintances, and even your old friends from high school. Develop a list and mail out something, then give them a quick call. Maybe you're a travel agent or you're selling cars or computers or home furnishings or stocks and bonds—things that everyone needs and everyone buys sooner or later. Family and friends become the first customers for many salespeople and you build from there.

But even if you are selling jet airplanes or complex software, let everyone know what you do. Just because you are selling something your friends and family know nothing about or have no direct connection to does not mean they cannot introduce you to people they know who need your products or services.

REMAIN POSITIVE

Positive people generate positive energy, which ultimately attracts customers, colleagues, and opportunities. Negativity bogs people down, saps their energy, and drives people away. Stay away from negative people. They have no value in your life.

With customers, you should always be positive. If someone asks how your business is going, say it is unbelievable. You could be just steps away from bankruptcy, but you have to present a positive outlook. This extends to your competition. Never badmouth your rivals. Mudslinging will never help you win your customer. It probably will only backfire.

If you're having trouble maintaining a positive outlook, you can find plenty of inspirational books, audio recordings, and web sites to improve your outlook. For starters, visit Mr. Positive himself, my friend and colleague Dave Boufford at www.mrpositive.com. SimpleTruths also offers some inspirational movies, including *212° The Extra Degree,* which you can check out at www.simpletruths .com/movies. Get yourself pumped up and stay that way! This can make a huge difference in your career.

WORK FOR TODAY, TOMORROW, AND YOUR FUTURE

As a salesperson, you are probably very busy attending to today's business, but if that is all you are attending to, then you are merely *doing* business, not *building a business.* This is a common trap, and it often results in a sales career that is less successful and more stressful than it really needs to be. You end up constantly chasing your tail—hunting for new clients one day, serving them the next, and starting the whole cycle over again the following day. Every month, it's either feast or famine.

To avoid having a sales career marked with slumps and spikes that burns you out long before you hit your stride, always be working on today's business, tomorrow's business, and future business. Take some time every day to sow the seeds of tomorrow's and your future business, so you will always have plenty of business to harvest. This will take you off the sales roller coaster that destroys both the personal and professional lives of so many salespeople.

By taking this approach, you can flatten out the hills and valleys and establish a steady flow of business and revenue. You can plan your business and scale your workforce more effectively, so you are not in a constant cycle of hiring people and then laying them off. You and your team will be much happier and more productive.

Tip: *Remember your ABCs and Ds.* A projects are those that need immediate attention and that are very close to generating revenue. B projects are in the works. C projects are in the planning stage. And D projects are those you have just begun considering. Keep clearing those As off your plate, moving Bs to As, Cs to Bs, and Ds to Cs (or delete the Ds that are not worth pursuing or that you know will never move up the ladder). With this system in place, you can always be sure that you are working on today's business, tomorrow's business, and future business.

STICK TO IT

Very likely you have heard the expression: It is always darkest before the dawn. Everybody knows that expression, yet it fails to encourage many people to stick with it. Time and time again, I see very skilled professionals give up just before they are about to achieve success. They get discouraged, run out of steam, and collapse right before they cross the finish line.

Remember: If you keep working hard, things will improve.

I coined a word for this: *sticktoitism.* You're probably already familiar with the word stick-to-itiveness. That is the official word— the one you will find in most dictionaries. I prefer my version, and I prefer it so much that I am determined it will earn its place in the dictionary some day. In short, sticktoitism is the dogged determination required to get something done in the face of adversity.

You need to make a commitment to yourself, right here and right now to be a successful salesperson. Promise yourself that no obstacle will block you from your goal and that you will continue to pursue your goal regardless of how impossible the odds of success seem to be. If you honor that commitment, I can guarantee that you will achieve whatever level of success you are capable of dreaming for yourself because you will not let up until you have achieved it.

My friend John Vigi became one of the nation's top stockbrokers, but when he started out, he had no clients and no commissions. John remembers cold-calling as many as 300 people in a row without a single sale. Talk about discouraging! His secret of success, however, is no secret. He had the sticktoitism required to succeed, and succeed he did.

His determination and sticktoitism brought the attention of Merrill Lynch leadership and he was promoted and celebrated by his company many times over. During his time at Merrill Lynch, his portfolio of clients kept him busy enough to be among Merrill Lynch's top brokers nationwide. For me it's the same. I don't have to work nearly as hard at selling as I once did. I've established my customer base and hired great assistants. Now I have an ever-growing business along with more time to pursue my professional and personal goals, more time for family and community and myself.

Stick to it, and you will succeed.

Ralph's Rule: If you are a novice, remember this: Even the most successful producers started out alone and afraid, but you can overcome this with natural curiosity, hard work, and savvy marketing. Ask questions, work hard, and let everyone know who you are, what you do, and what you sell.

WEEK 2

STAY PUT

High turnover among staff can kill any business, from fast food to the biggest corporations. I believe it is especially damaging to sales organizations. Believe me, I tried it both ways—jumping from job to job and staying put—and I know from experience that staying put definitely is better for me, my customers, and my company.

I have observed that most salespeople jump from company to company hoping for a better commission split or a nicer boss or better hours. I did that myself when I was younger. I changed real estate firms seven or eight times, always hoping for a better arrangement, before I finally opened my own company. I realize now how silly I was to think all that moving around would have done me any good.

It is clear to me now that the perfect boss, the perfect company, and the ideal marketplace are nothing more than seductive illusions. You make money by digging deep where you are right now and making it happen here and now. The only thing that switching from firm to firm accomplishes is to waste your time, energy, and resources and significantly damage your bottom line and the bottom line of the company whose products you have been selling.

Just imagine how much burden the departure of a skilled and experienced salesperson can place on a company. New salespeople are not nearly as productive. In addition, the company now needs to invest more resources training someone new, and the new person is much more likely to make costly mistakes. Of course, when you are a disgruntled salesperson, the damage that your departure does to the company is no concern of yours—in fact, their loss can make you feel even better about leaving.

However, when you choose to leave, you experience similar setbacks. You lose some of your business contacts and support from colleagues. You are not nearly as productive learning new products and new systems as you would be selling for a company where you already know the ropes. And in your new position, you are more likely to commit costly mistakes. Bottom line: You will have fewer transactions, and each transaction will take you longer to process, at least until you can get up to speed. One more thing to consider: There is no guarantee that you will be treated any better or have better opportunities at this new company.

In contrast, an experienced staff requires much less supervision. In auto sales, veterans often perform double the number of transactions per month as their novice counterparts, and top producers may do 30 or more transactions a month—a sale a day! Veterans also need only one hour per deal instead of the four hours a transaction typically takes a novice to process. Quite a savings for the dealership, and quite a boost in earnings potential for salespeople who stay put.

Every time I moved to a new company, I had to start over. Every time I switched real estate firms, I had to buy new business cards and let my clients know where they could find me. I had to create new stationery. I had to develop new marketing materials. Each time, I lost a lot of momentum. And, of course, I had to learn a whole new system with each new company.

Was it worth it? No, it wasn't. In hindsight I think it's clear that all those moves cost me more money than they made me.

Sometimes you'll have a serious disagreement with your boss. You may have different goals for yourself than your boss does. If these disagreements are serious enough, then, yes perhaps you ought to make a move. But don't give in to that temptation to move every time you run into a routine disappointment at the office. Instead, take some of that energy and put it into making things better where you are.

Perhaps you can negotiate a different commission split or get your boss to pay for new marketing material for you. Maybe your company will pay to get you some additional training or to send you to your industry's annual convention. Any of these steps would make you a more professional salesperson and probably a happier person. It would ease the disappointment that was making you consider moving on.

Try it next time you're tempted to move. What can you lose? If it doesn't work, you can always go somewhere else. But you may find that your working conditions and/or pay improve just for the asking.

In Week 3, I show you how to develop an entrepreneurial mindset that will ultimately place you in control of your own destiny regardless of external influences, such as what your sales manager says or does or doesn't say or do.

Ralph's Rule: The most successful salespeople are the ones who make things happen where they are, not the ones who jump ship to new companies every year, hoping to find happiness somewhere else.

WEEK 3

CULTIVATE AN ENTREPRENEURIAL MINDSET

T oo many salespeople think of themselves as employ-ees, treat their careers as jobs, and focus too much on market conditions. They bellyache about the dealer or broker they work for, their sales manager who provides no support, the unrealistic sales quotas they have to meet, and the fact that the economy just isn't what it used to be. They end up wasting a lot of time they could be using to move more product. As long as a salesperson has a mindset that what they are doing for a living is a job, they will be in a dead-end job.

To be successful in sales, stop thinking like an order-taker and start thinking like a small-business owner, an entrepreneur. Think of yourself as You, Inc., a business entity unto yourself, a revenue generator. Your success depends on you and you alone.

PROCURE TOOLS AND RESOURCES

Take a few minutes to write down a comprehensive list of what you think you need to succeed in sales. Do you need a new computer? A specialized software program? A way to market yourself more efficiently in print or on the Internet? An assistant to fill out paper-work? Additional training? Draw up a comprehensive list of tools and resources you need, prioritize the items on your list, estimate the cost of each item, and then start gathering everything you need.

Tip: If you have a sales manager, you may be able to convince your manager to cover the cost of some of the items you need or at least offset your cost in some way.

By performing this exercise, you are essentially creating a business plan for You, Inc. You probably already have a clear idea of what success would look like for you. Now you are developing a plan for moving from point A (where you are now) to point B (where you will be when you have achieved success). I talk more about goals in Week 5 and about developing a comprehensive plan in Week 6.

Your business plan should contain a timetable, estimated costs, and your estimated increase in sales revenue. It may even include how much time you are initially willing to invest per week and how much time you will spend each week maintaining that level of success once you achieve it. Consider including a breakeven point in your timetable, showing exactly when you anticipate the investment to pay for itself.

If you are an independent sales agent or if your manager refuses to invest in your success, then acquire the resources you need yourself. Borrow the money if you have to. Invest in your own success.

Tip: Demonstrate your commitment to the company you work for before expecting the company to demonstrate a commitment to your success. Once you have proven yourself, you hold a stronger position at the negotiating table.

Remember: The great thing about sales success is that you invest time and energy up front, but once you achieve success, maintaining it requires much less time and effort. You can then invest your extra free time and energy in other pursuits, both professional and personal. You can achieve a balanced life, which is ultimately much more rewarding and fulfilling than career success alone.

MARKET YOURSELF

Now that you are your own business, launch it like any large corporation might launch a new brand. I often observe salespeople primarily marketing the companies they work for and only secondarily marketing themselves. They pitch themselves as RE/MAX agents or Ford dealers rather than emphasizing their own brand. When you crank up the marketing machinery, keep in mind that You, Inc. is the company you are promoting.

You may be marketing your company and your products, but those entities are only peripheral interests. You include them because they are a part of what you sell, but by marketing yourself, you ensure long-term success. Even if you happen to change companies or start selling other products, you retain all the benefits of the time, money, and energy you invested in your marketing efforts.

Tip: Before clients will buy *from* you, they have to buy *into* you. They have to know you and trust you, know what you sell, and believe that you are going to treat them fairly and with respect. The goal of your marketing campaign should always be to build a high positive profile that constantly reinforces your image and the fact that you are knowledgeable and trustworthy.

Your personal marketing campaign should exploit all media, including print advertising (business cards, flyers, brochures, and so on), the Internet (web sites, blogs, e-mail, e-newsletters, and so on), and traditional media (television, radio, newspapers, and magazines). In Week 17, I show you how to engage in shameless self-promotion. However, remember that this is not an ego trip. Your success depends entirely on your ability to make your customers and everyone around you successful, too.

HIRE EMPLOYEES (ASSISTANTS)

Until you have one or more employees, you are simply a self-employed freelancer, and you are probably wasting time on no- or low-profit chores, such as pushing paper and stuffing envelopes. You should be spending time on dollar-productive activities—marketing yourself, meeting with clients, selling product, and exploring other revenue-generating opportunities and partnerships. Everything else you should delegate to your assistants.

I always tell the people whom I mentor or coach, "If you don't have an assistant, you are one." If you don't have an assistant, hire at least one. If you are concerned about having to handle payroll, consider hiring a virtual assistant (VA) who works on contract. That way, you can pay the person, issue him or her a form 1099 at the end of the year, and not have to worry about dealing with complicated payroll deductions. In Week 8, I unlock the secret to my success—the people who help me achieve what I could never achieve on my own.

BUILD A SALES TEAM

When more business is coming in than you can personally handle yourself, consider building your own sales team rather than turning away prospective clients. You can handle the arrangement any way you wish. You may include someone, probably yourself, who plays the role of rain maker—attracting new business; another person who takes care of the actual selling of product; and a third person in charge of closing the deal and processing the paperwork. Each person on the team can have his or her own specialty.

As business picks up, you can add members to the team to scale up for the increased workload and acquire talent the team is lacking. Always be in the process of recruiting new talent, and take your time adding members to the team, so you can add the cream of the crop.

Admittedly, any discussion of building a sales team is premature for Week 3, but I want you to break out of the habit of thinking small and break into the habit of thinking and living large. You need to realize early on that your potential is unlimited. In Week 47, we will revisit the team concept, so you can begin planning your sales team as next year's project.

Ralph's Rule: Winners make sales. Losers make excuses. You are the key to your own success.

WEEK 4

PROJECT A POSITIVE ATTITUDE

P ositive things happen to positive people. While you might question what came first, the positive attitude or the positive things, the fact is that negativity drains ambition and motivation, and without motivation, you never even get up off the couch to try anything.

I have witnessed with my own eyes the destructive power of negativity. I have seen productive staffs fall victim to a single Eyeore who was convinced that nothing good would ever come his way. Both negativity and positivity (yes, I made up that word) are contagious. The question is: Which one would you prefer to catch and have your team catch?

Good things usually do not "just happen," but the more positive you are and the harder you work to make good things happen, the more likely good things will start to happen. As with almost everything in life, the first step is the most important, and the first step is to foster a positive attitude in yourself. This chapter shows you how.

SURROUND YOURSELF WITH POSITIVE PEOPLE

Henry Ford once said, "Whether you think you can or whether you think you can't, you're right." The first step toward success is to believe you can. I think that most people are born with this belief because without it, most people would never learn to crawl, walk, or talk.

Unfortunately, over time, many people have their can-do attitudes trained right out of them—their dreams trampled by people who encourage them to be "realistic" and set their expectations low in order to avoid disappointment. Discouraged in their youth, these people tend to discourage others when they become adults.

On the other hand, people who've been encouraged to pursue their dreams tend to encourage others. They see problems not as insurmountable obstacles, but as challenges that can be overcome. They focus on the goal and do whatever it takes to achieve it.

When you surround yourself with positive people, you have a support group and fan club all rolled into one. They cheer you on through disappointment, assist you with their skills and experience, and share their resources to help you achieve your goals.

SEEK OUT POSITIVE IDEAS

In 1952, Norman Vincent Peale published *The Power of Positive Thinking*, which was destined to become an international bestseller. The notion that you could transform your life by transforming your thoughts was revolutionary, and readers loved to hear the message that they were the masters of their own destiny.

Motivational books, audio recordings, and even videos abound. You can find them at your local bookstore, on the Internet at sites such as www.simpletruths.com, and by attending motivational seminars. All of these resources are great tools for boosting your enthusiasm and energy and establishing a healthy and productive mindset. Throughout my career, I have actively sought out motivational speakers and writers for inspiration.

In my youth, when most of my generation was following the adventures of Superman and Wonder Woman, I had entirely different heroes, including Zig Ziglar, Tom Hopkins, and Charlie "Tremendous" Jones. I read their books. I listened to their tapes. I even skipped school to attend their events and rallies. I didn't have enough money to get in, so I would have to go to the place they were speaking at 5:30 AM to sneak in.

I wouldn't hesitate to approach these incredible speakers. I was awestruck, but I would approach them after the event and ask questions or tell them how much I admired them. Zig Ziglar once asked a young Ralph Roberts, "What are you doing here, son?" I gushed out, "I got special permission to be here, sir," I lied. "Someday I'm going to be successful like you and do what you do." "I'm sure you will," he said.

His words were inspirational. What an incredible moment for me. Luckily, I wasn't afraid to approach and talk to these people. Today, I invite many speakers to come to the Detroit area for lunch. Those I'm friends with, I invite to visit with my family. I get to network with these inspirational and intelligent people. You won't believe how much you can learn and how inspiring their enthusiasm can be.

BANISH NEGATIVITY AND SELF-DEFEATISM

Whenever I'm talking on the phone and the person on the other end starts to go negative on me, I make an excuse to end the call. I'm not rude about it. I just say something like, "Hey, I have another call coming in, can I call you right back?"

This short-circuits the negativity and gives me some time to regroup and set the conversation back on a more positive track. When I call back 15 minutes, an hour, or a day later, I can then begin the conversation on a positive note and hopefully keep it moving forward in the right direction.

I make a point of not letting negativity in. If I sense it, I immediately find a way to steer clear of it, just as I would veer to the left or right to avoid an oncoming car. It's as instinctive to me as the fight or flight response. Negative self-talk and self-defeatist thinking can be as destructive to your goals as a head-on collision, so I strongly encourage you to avoid them at all costs.

MASTER THE ART OF POSITIVE TALK

The first date I ever went on with my wife, Kathy, was to lunch at a local pancake house. I had met Kathy when I was running one of my sports bars and she and her girlfriends came in. At first she didn't seem very interested in me. I tried to spark her interest in various ways without much success. Then, after talking on the phone a few times, I finally said that we should have lunch at the pancake house, and would she like me to pick her up or meet me there? And that's what finally got us going together.

Notice I didn't ask Kathy, "Would you like to have lunch with me?" My question assumed we were having lunch, and the only question was how to get there. This is an example of asking for something in a way that assumes a positive outcome. I've heard this technique called "power talking" and various other terms. It's a tried-and-true sales technique. For example, when a waitress asks, "Would you like a glass of red or white?" instead of "Would you like a glass of wine?" But, like most of the techniques in this book, it's one that too many salespeople ignore.

Recently, on a very busy day when I hardly had time to think, a reporter began a telephone interview with me asking if she could tape record our conversation. Instead of just saying, "Yes, that's okay," I replied, "Get out your tape recorder and let's have some fun!" She laughed and I could just feel her energy level rising. The interview continued on this higher level of energy, and that, of course, resulted in a more positive story for me.

Basically, positive talking is a way to emphasize common ground, to create positive thinking, and to get both sides working toward a successful outcome. It's a way to express your interest in you client's well-being. It's a way to energize a situation. Just think about how the singing of the National Anthem before a baseball game energizes the crowd. You need that same quick uplift in energy when you begin a sales call. Positive talking can help you get that.

Picture this: Suppose you go into a meeting after a long, difficult day. You're grouchy, tired, and you don't really want to be there. When your host says, "How are you?" you could be bluntly honest and say what kind of a day you've had. Or you could say, "Great! And this meeting will make my day even better." The second version is more likely to lift your own spirits and put everyone in the mood to do business.

Note the distinction between this upbeat, forward-looking style of conversing and a reliance on scripts or other phony approaches. You can't rely on scripted remarks without putting off your clients. They can tell when you're not sincere. Positive talking doesn't mean being phony or dishonest or manipulative.

Rather, being positive assumes you still react honestly to any given situation but you remain confident, focused, and engaged with the client in your conversational style. Positive talking is a way of conversing that increases the energy level for both you and your client, while negative talking drains that energy. Positive talking alone won't win you a new client, but the lack of it will lose you many.

Ralph's Rule: Pay careful attention to your conversational style with clients. Ask yourself this: Would you want to do business with you? Customers like salespeople who are positive and professional and who make them feel special. Positive talking can help you achieve this image.

WEEK 5

SET GOALS

S etting a goal is like choosing a vacation destination and date of departure. It keeps you focused. It forces you to plan ahead. It dictates what you need to do to get from point A to point B, enjoy yourself at point B, and return home.

Most of us are good at planning our vacations. When it comes to planning our days, weeks, months, years, businesses, or careers, however, we run into all sorts of problems. We wander around aimlessly. We look back at the past five years and realize that we have gone nowhere. We take inventory and can recall no major accomplishments.

The cause is usually due to a lack of planning, and planning cannot take place until you have a destination—a specific goal—in mind. How could you effectively plan a vacation, for example, if you have no idea whether you're traveling to New York, Beijing, or Nairobi and no set date of departure or arrival? You would have no idea what to pack. You could not arrange your flights or reserve a room. You would not even know whether you needed a passport! Yet, this is exactly how many professionals, including salespeople, approach their careers.

In this chapter, I show you how to take control of your own destiny by setting goals and then setting yourself on a course to achieve those goals.

ASSOCIATE WITH FELLOW GOAL SETTERS

In sales as in any other field of endeavor, people generally fall into four categories in terms of goal setting:

1. People who set goals and deadlines and try to achieve them.
2. People who set goals and deadlines and never follow through on them.
3. People who don't set goals or deadlines.
4. People who refuse to set goals or deadlines and look down on those who do.

To achieve the greatest level of success in the least amount of time, I strongly encourage you to become a member of the first group and associate with fellow goal setters. As you discovered in Week 4, people can drag you down, and this applies to goal setting. Anyone who's critical of goal setting or rolls their eyes whenever you mention the topic will only weaken your enthusiasm and resolve.

Remember: Misery loves company. Failure loves company, too. Refuse to allow those who are committed to failure and misery drag you down with them.

SET A GOAL

A goal is generally anything you want to do (a process goal) or anything you want to achieve or be (a production goal). I encourage you to set both types of goals, as explained in the following sections.

Process Goals

I firmly believe in processes and procedures. If you develop a foolproof process, have competent people in place, and give them the resources they need, you can guarantee consistent delivery of a quality product or service.

The same can be applied to you as an individual. For example, I can almost guarantee that top-notch salespeople will significantly boost sales by making 100 phone calls a day, as you will discover in Week 22. This is an example of a *process goal*.

Process goals may seem more like commitments than goals to you, but I consider them goals. And the great thing about them is that they place you in total control of achieving the goal.

Production Goals

Production goals are often directly linked to your process goals. For example, a process goal of making 100 phone calls per day is almost guaranteed to result in boosting sales (a production goal). For example, you may set a production goal of increasing sales 25 percent or selling 200 cars or 150 houses or X number of whatever you sell per year.

Production goals are useful in setting a bar for yourself and measuring your relative productivity from one period to another. However, you need to be careful not to focus on productivity to the point of damaging your sales technique or future business. For example, if you become pushy trying to meet a sales goal or are too willing to cut a deal with a client to make a sale, your productivity goal could work against you. In addition, if you are so focused on making this month's sales numbers that you fail to work on building your future business, you could be sacrificing long-term success for short-term success.

I do encourage you, however, to set production goals. After all, as salespeople, how much we sell is often our measure of success. Either you make your numbers or you don't.

SET A DEADLINE

Goals without deadlines are meaningless. Claiming that you will earn $1 million means nothing without a time frame. Whether you earn it over the course of a decade, a year, a month, or a day makes a big difference. In addition, without a deadline, you have no motivation—time needs to be nipping at your heels.

In some cases, the deadline may be set for you. For example, your manager may set a sales quota for you that you are expected to meet for the year, quarter, or month. If your company does not set a goal for you and specify a deadline, then do it yourself. Set a deadline that is realistic but challenging—a deadline that will motivate you to take action and spur you on to achieve great things.

BREAK DOWN YOUR GOAL INTO MILESTONES

A challenging goal can often seem overwhelming at first. When I set a goal to sell 300 homes in a year, it seemed a little unrealistic until I broke it down. I would need to sell about 25 homes per month or 6 per week. This still seemed a little overwhelming, so I broke it down even further. I could sell 4 FSBOs (For Sale By Owner properties) per month, 6 expired listings, and 8 foreclosures. That was 18, meaning I would need to secure only 7 more traditional listings per month. Now my goal of selling 300 homes in a year seemed more doable.

Making your goals as simple as possible makes them more attainable. It also helps you identify bottlenecks that could be keeping you from your goal. When I decided to sell 300 homes in a year, for example, I soon realized that my current approach did not enable me to have the number of showings I would need to achieve that goal. That led to an innovative solution—take more than one set of buyers on showings.

I also identified another bottleneck—I could not possibly process all the paperwork required for 300 transactions. I knew I would need assistance, so I hired people to process the paperwork for me.

By breaking the goal into milestones and identifying areas where I needed to improve, I could make a seemingly impossible goal possible.

Ralph's Rule: Set goals for each day, week, month, and year; prioritize tasks to achieve your goals; review your goals at the end of each period; celebrate your achievements; and rework your goals when you fall short of achieving them.

WEEK 6

DEVISE A PLAN

E ven if you act as a sales representative (rep) for a company, you are a business unto yourself. You have or should have your own income (in the form of commissions) and expenses. Like a bona fide business, you may even have separate budgets for marketing and operations, and if you have one or more assistants (and you should), you also have a payroll.

As a business, you should have your own business plan. A business plan does not have to be an intricately detailed document, but it does require a substantial amount of thought and foresight. It needs to address the structure of your business, what it does, and where it wants to ultimately end up. Your business plan establishes early on that what you are creating is an entity unto itself—something that's bigger than just you and that ideally should continue to exist when you're ready to retire or move on to something else.

ESSENTIAL ELEMENTS OF A BUSINESS PLAN

You can find loads of books and other resources on developing business plans that go into far more detail than I can possibly cover in one short chapter. I encourage you to reference one or more of these comprehensive resources at some point in your career. For now, focus on the basics covered in this chapter, and make sure your business plan does the following:

- Describes your business.
- Defines your market.
- Analyzes the situation.
- Communicates your vision.
- Projects revenue.
- Budgets for expenses.
- Identifies sources of investment capital.

Next I offer some additional guidance on how to develop each section of your business plan.

BUSINESS DESCRIPTION

Every business plan should start with a brief description of the business and what it does, for example:

> As a business-to-business sales company, I am dedicated to assisting customers in selecting and using the right packaging products and services for their distribution needs.

Although the description is relatively brief (25 words), it sets out exactly what the business will do and what it offers clients.

MARKET FOCUS

Next, your business plan must establish your market, and by that, I do not mean something broad like "the housing market" or "the auto industry." Although it may seem irrational, you have a better chance of achieving success by narrowing your market focus.

Instead of taking aim at the entire residential real estate market, for example, you may want to focus initially on first-time buyers or on people who are relocating to the area or retirees who need to downsize. Instead of trying to sell furniture to everyone within 20 miles of your store, you may want to focus on upscale homeowners or middle-income families. You can always expand later, but it's best to start out with a limited focus.

Following is a sample market analysis for someone who sells athletic shoes and accessories:

> The athletic shoes and accessories I sell are for competitive runners in high-school, collegiate, and Olympic arenas located on the West Coast of the United States. This market is willing to spend more on high-quality athletic gear that is proven to increase performance.

SITUATION ANALYSIS

Businesses are never created in a vacuum, so your business plan needs to address the realities of where you plan on doing business. It should address questions, such as the following:

- What makes you uniquely capable of achieving success in this market?
- What relationships can you tap for additional leverage?
- Who are your top competitors?
- Are you facing any additional challenges due to current market conditions?
- How is the market likely to change in the future?

Your business plan should have an entire section devoted exclusively to analyzing the current situation. Here's an example of what a pharmaceutical salesperson might include in his or her business plan:

> With over 10 years of experience in selling prescription medications for several different pharmaceutical companies, I now have a broad knowledge of various product lines and specific products that are currently available. Through my high-level contacts at local hospitals, I can market directly to most local area physicians and gain broad distribution through local pharmacies.
>
> XYZ is my main competitor, but the company has a reputation for not delivering on time and failing to provide doctors with sufficient samples. By providing exceptional service 24/7, I am confident that I can capture at least 50 percent of XYZ's existing market share.

VISION STATEMENT

When you close your eyes and imagine how your ideal business will operate, what do you see yourself doing on a daily basis? This vision should be included in your business plan. Your vision is likely to touch on other components of your business plan, including your market, the consumers you are targeting, and the unique combination of products and services you have to offer. In your vision, you crystallize everything in your business plan, summing up everything in a brief paragraph of two to five sentences, such as:

> As the MPG guy, I specialize in sales and service of high-mileage vehicles of all makes and models in the highly green-aware community of Denver, Colorado. I offer only high-performance vehicles with proven track records for high-mileage and low emissions and work closely with customers to choose the right vehicle for their budget and lifestyle. After-sale service is a high-priority to ensure customer satisfaction long after the sale.

REVENUE PROJECTIONS

I often tell the salespeople and business owners I coach to forget about the bottom line and focus on the top line—your clients. Customer service should always be your primary focus, but when you are developing a business plan, you must pay some attention to your bottom line. Your business plan should include the following:

- Gross revenue you need to generate in order to break even, both annually and monthly. (Once you calculate your expenses, as discussed in the following section, you will have a clearer idea of your breakeven point.)
- The gross revenue you plan to earn both annually and monthly—your revenue goal.
- The number of transactions you need to complete in order to generate that revenue.
- The average commission from each transaction.

Many of the details you include in your business plan are going to flow out of these initial estimates. For example, if you plan on expanding gross sales from $2.5 million to $5 million, your plan will need to include details on how you are going to accomplish that goal. Are you going to invest more resources in marketing? Will you need to hire additional personnel to process transactions and serve customers? Are you going to implement new technologies to increase productivity? Your revenue projections generate the questions that the rest of your business plan will need to answer.

BUDGET

In order for you to remain solvent, you have to create a business plan that sets you on a course of bringing in at least enough revenue to cover expenses. Consider breaking your expenses into three categories:

1. *One-time expenses or start-up costs:* One-time expenses include the cost of equipment, such as a building, car, computers, and office furniture. What do you need to get up and running?

2. *Fixed monthly expenses:* These are hard expenses that will change little if at all each year. They will be a line item on your budget. Some of them might include rent or mortgage payment on your office building, taxes on your building, salaries, utility bills, phone service, Internet service, and office supplies.

3. *Fluctuating monthly expenses:* Some expenses are tough to pin down and budget for, including marketing and advertising expenses, seminars, and thank-you gifts. The good news is that you can usually cut back on fluctuating monthly expenses, if the need arises.

Your business plan needs to show how much money you need to bring in to get going and to keep going on a monthly and yearly basis.

START-UP MONEY

If you are already well-established, you may have sufficient funds and income to finance the implementation of your business plan yourself. If you are just starting out or are not quite successful enough yet to finance your future success, you may need to beg, borrow, or partner for the money and resources you need. Here are some ideas:

- Borrow money from family members or friends until you can "get on your feet."
- Borrow money from a bank or other lending institution.

- Barter your services for the products and services you need. (Consult your accountant to determine whether you need to pay taxes on these trades.)

- Establish a partnership with someone who has what you need and needs what you have. (Be careful, though; partnerships can be very tricky and somewhat risky. I used to say "Pick a partner as carefully as you pick a spouse," but with divorce rates at about 50 percent, I'm beginning to think that you need to pick a partner more carefully than most people choose a spouse.)

Do not hesitate to borrow the money you need to get started. Not starting is worse. Assuming you have a solid plan in place and you work the plan, you should have no problem paying back the loans.

Ralph's Rule: Plan your work and then work your plan. When theory (your plan) encounters reality, you will often notice flaws in your plan. Make the necessary adjustments and keep trying until you get it right. Far too many salespeople abandon their plans at the first sign of trouble, which is usually a big mistake. When a ship is drifting off course, the captain does not turn around and head back; changing course a couple degrees is usually all that is required.

WEEK 7

DEVELOP SYSTEMS AND PROCEDURES

S ystems can set you free.
I have proven this fact time and time again with the systems I created over the course of my career. Early on, I had a system in place for covering my floor time at the real estate office where I worked. I hired an assistant to answer the phones and take messages for me instead of doing it myself. This freed me up to spend more time with my clients.

Later, I developed a system that enabled me to show homes to more than one couple at a time and have the paperwork processed on the way back to the office after couples finally decided on a home. By developing systems and procedures for processing the paperwork, I could outsource the job to assistants, again giving me more time to do what I do best and love most—sell to clients.

When I decided to expand operations into acquiring foreclosure properties, I developed a system for that, as well. In fact, I wrote a step-by-step procedure manual complete with sample documents that enabled any intelligent individual to profit from the purchase and sale of homes in preforeclosure. I then hired someone to run my "foreclosure division." I still became involved in certain transactions, but the talented and gifted team I put together handled most of the work, so I was free to deal with higher-level issues.

Systems have set me free, and they can do the same for you.

DOCUMENT YOUR JOB

Salespeople often convince themselves that nobody can do what they do as well as they do it. As a result, they end up wasting time performing routine tasks that any fully trained assistant could do just as well. Even worse, because they waste time on routine tasks, they have less time and energy to devote to customers who really need it.

In our book *Power Teams: The Complete Guide to Building and Managing a Winning Real Estate Agent Team*, RISMedia's founder and CEO John Featherston and I point out the many benefits of the team-based approach to sales. One of the top benefits is that sales teams excel in providing customer service, because other members of the team liberate the salesperson so he or she can focus on tasks that only the salesperson is qualified to perform.

Before you become too convinced that nobody could do what you do as well as you do it, I challenge you to document everything you do. Create a step-by-step procedure manual for all the tasks you perform. If you take up the challenge, I am convinced that you will discover that you are wasting time on many tasks you could easily outsource to an assistant—anything from assembling marketing and sales packets to screening your e-mail to filling out sales reports to building and maintaining your web site.

As an added bonus, if you take up my challenge, you now have a detailed procedure manual for training your assistant. With step-by-step procedures and a little hands-on training, your assistant can be up and running in less than a week. All you have to do is delegate, and the more experienced your assistant becomes, the less training you'll need to provide.

Tip: If you do not want to spend time writing procedures manuals, then consider hiring a technical writer to do it for you. The technical writer can help you identify procedures, break them into tasks, and then write step-by-step instructions. Including sample documents or boilerplates, so your assistant can simply "fill in the blanks", can take a lot of the guesswork out of some tasks.

IDENTIFY PROCEDURES

The first step is to identify procedures. Real estate agents might have a procedures list that looks something like this:

- Send out a marketing packet.
- Send out a prelisting packet.
- Color-code files.
- Follow up with clients.
- Process transactions.
- Develop a sales presentation to deliver to sellers.
- Develop a sales presentation to deliver to buyers.
- Assemble a preclosing packet.

If you're selling automobiles, tractors, computers, pharmaceuticals, lawn-care services, or any other products or services, your procedures list is likely to look quite a bit different. Sit down with a pad of paper and a pen, and start jotting down a list of procedures to follow when dealing with new clients. This should help you identify the procedures you already follow to make a sale.

Break Procedures into Tasks

Once you have a set of procedures, break each procedure into a series of tasks. Your goal is to make each procedure as easy to accomplish as possible, so you do not have to answer questions or show a new hire what to do. You simply show the person where the procedures manuals and any required tools and supplies are located. The new employee or team member can then follow the required steps.

For example, the procedure for sending out a marketing packet to a prospective client may require your assistant to perform the following tasks:

- Write a personalized letter or note to the client.
- Gather the latest marketing materials.
- Drop the packet off at the prospective client's home.

Breaking procedures into tasks enables your assistants to execute the procedures with very little room for error. It also allows you to break things down, so they don't seem so overwhelming.

Break Tasks into Steps

Break each task into steps. You may even want to illustrate the steps. For example, you may include in your training manual one or two sample letters to clients, so a new hire has a model letter for guidance.

Don't forget to include Yes/No decision steps. Your assistant may have to make a decision at some point in the process, and then follow one set of instructions if the answer is Yes and a different set of instructions if the answer is No.

DELEGATE THE WORK

Once your procedures are in place and you have one or more assistants, as discussed in Week 8, "Hire an Assistant," you can start focusing on what you do best and delegating the rest. Delegating becomes a matter of simply finding something that needs to be done and handing it off to the person most qualified and best trained to accomplish the task.

Now you have no excuse for not having enough time to "get around to it." Do it, delegate it, or ditch it.

Ralph's Rule: Train your assistants well, provide them with the equipment and resources they need to perform their jobs, and then give them the freedom and responsibility to do their jobs. We salespeople tend to be control freaks, and this can drive your best people right out the door.

WEEK 8

HIRE AN ASSISTANT

About 30 years ago, when I was just a kid starting out in sales, I hired a high school student to answer the phones for me after school. I still remember what a relief it was to have her handle the routine calls while I concentrated on doing what I do best—working with buyers and sellers.

After I had gained some experience and had more revenue flowing in, I added a secretary. Later I hired an assistant to handle my investment properties and another to help me with my closings. In time I delegated big chunks of my operation to assistants—marketing specialists, an in-house lawyer, my own CPA, and many, many more. These people represented my attempts to duplicate myself so that I could accomplish even more. Believe me, I could not possibly have handled the volume I was doing at the time without my dedicated group of assistants.

You cannot do it all by yourself, but this is exactly the approach many salespeople try when they want to sell more goods and services: They work harder and put in more hours. Eventually, they burn out. What they should be doing is adding personnel, at least one assistant to start. Hopefully, this chapter will convince you to hire your first (or next) assistant.

RECRUIT ASSISTANTS

I constantly recruit assistants and other talented individuals to become members of my team. After all, each person on my team is a revenue generator; the more revenue generators I have, the more profitable we become as a team. As long as you can manage your team's growth, you should always be in the process of recruiting new members, who can then generate more revenue for the team.

Tip: Don't focus your recruiting efforts solely on people in your industry. People in other industries, particularly those in customer-service positions, often make top recruits. You can teach new team members your business, but it is much tougher to teach them the people skills required to deal with clients.

Before approaching a prospective recruit, watch how the person interacts with others, including employees, colleagues, and the general public. Also observe how the person takes direction—is the person able to accept input and guidance while still being assertive with his or her own ideas or solutions? All these intangibles are more important than experience in your industry.

Network for Leads

When you start looking for a new assistant or other team member, tell everyone you know about the position you need to fill and the qualifications you're looking for. Your most trusted friends and associates may have someone in mind who would be a good fit. Don't rule out any sources for good leads. You can find qualified candidates at your car dealer, in a restaurant or hotel, or anywhere you can see people in action doing their jobs.

Tip: Even when you don't have an opening, continue your recruiting efforts. Whenever you meet new people, ask them what they do and ask for their business card or contact information and then add them to your address book. When a need arises, you will have a complete database of individuals to contact to start your search.

Advertise Openings

If you documented your job as I recommended you do in Week 7, you should already have a pretty good idea of which tasks you want to assign to an assistant. Now, use your notes to write a job description and pare it down a bit to create an advertisement for the opening. Be sure to ask qualified candidates to submit a cover letter and resume.

You can post your want ad in the usual places, such as the local newspaper, but consider advertising on the Web, as well, including the following sites:

- Monster at www.monster.com.
- Career Builder at www.careerbuilder.com.
- Craig's List at www.craigslist.org.
- Backpage.com at www.backpage.com.
- Google Base at base.google.com.

Consider contacting local colleges and high schools that have co-op programs. Many ambitious and talented high school students would jump at the opportunity to get real-world experience, and many of these "kids" have a great deal of technical know-how. I have hired high school students to do everything from planting For Sale signs to designing my web sites.

You can also locate virtual assistants with experience in the real estate industry by visiting any of the following sites (you will learn more about virtual assistants later in this chapter):

- International Virtual Assistants Association (IVAA) at www.ivaa.org.
- Real Estate Virtual Assistants (REVA) Network at www.revanetwork.com.
- Virtual Assistant Networking Association at www.virtualassistantnetworking.com.
- Virtual Real Estate Assistant (VREA) at vrea.com.

SCREEN THE CANDIDATES

After you have lined up a few promising candidates for a particular position, you have to assess their skills, personality, and character through skill assessments, interviews, and possibly even personality testing. In the following sections, I show you how to weed out the less promising candidates and zero in on the best of them.

Assess Skills and Experience

The first hurdle any candidate must clear is the skills and experience hurdle—the person must have the knowledge and skills required to do the job. If you need a personal assistant, for example, the right candidate must have excellent communications skills (written and verbal); be able to type and perform basic math; have some mastery of basic software, including a word processor, e-mail, and Web-based tools; and be able to answer phones, take messages, and manage your calendar.

To assess a candidate's knowledge and skills, I recommend you do the following:

- *Request transcripts.* If the person claims to have a degree or certification, request proof, usually in the form of transcripts.
- *Check references.* Have each candidate complete a job application complete with references, and then follow up by checking those references.
- *Test for the skills you need.* Create your own tests to assess skills such as typing, performing basic math, writing ad copy, and developing presentations. You might even have the person type a letter for you or design a spreadsheet. (It is best to have the person perform the test at your office, so they cannot have someone else take the test for them.)

Perform a DISC Assessment

I recommend that you subject yourself and every candidate you seriously consider hiring as an assistant to a DISC assessment. (You need to assess yourself first to determine which tasks you are best suited to taking on and which tasks you would be better off delegating to others.) The DISC assessment is a personality test that helps determine personality types:

- *Director:* Characterized by control, power, and assertiveness. Ds are bottom-line people. Common phrases you might hear from a D are, "Let's cut to the chase," or, "Just get it done." Others often perceive Ds as impatient and insensitive. Ds are typically in sales or leadership positions because they are strong closers and are result-oriented.

- *Influencer:* Influencers tend to be social butterflies—"the life of the party." Common phrases you might hear from an I are, "Ooh, here's an idea," or, "Are we having fun yet?" Is are perceived as emotional and energetic. They have great people skills and gravitate toward sales and other positions with high profiles and frequent recognition opportunities.

- *Supporter:* Patience, persistence, and thoughtfulness required to carry out a task that supports the work of others. Ss are the nurturers and relaters; they live to serve and please others. They thrive on predictability, comfort and security. Common phrases you might hear from an S are, "Are you sure that's safe?" "Whatever makes you happy," or, "Whatever you think is best." Ss are perceived as protective and supportive. They tend to gravitate toward positions with low risk or long-term stability that offer an opportunity to help others.

- *Critical analyst:* Structured and organized mind; tends to be very analytical and good at solving problems. Cs are perfectionists; they crave and thrive on order and process. Common phrases you might hear from a C are, "I need more information before I can make a decision," or, "Getting it 100 percent right is far more important than how quickly it gets done." Cs are perceived as analytical, critical, and inflexible. Cs gravitate toward positions that require great attention to detail, thoroughness, and accuracy.

Generally speaking, people who are directors or influencers are usually better at working with people—managing other team members and dealing with customers. Supporters and critical analysts are better equipped at completing specific tasks and solving day-to-day problems. These are your behind-the-scenes people, who make sure the office runs smoothly and transactions are processed correctly and efficiently.

Every individual has a little D, I, S, and C, but one of the four personality types tends to be more prominent than the others. The DISC assessment helps identify each candidate's most prominent personality type. Employers who use the DISC assessment find that it helps cut down significantly on turnover, because they can hire the person who's the right fit from the very start.

Caution: People have a tendency to hire others who have personalities similar to their own. This could be a big mistake. If you hire a director type to be your assistant, you could have a serious power struggle on your hands. Hire the right personality for the right position. The DISC assessment can help.

Administer the Assessment

My colleague and friend Howard Brinton of Star Power Systems (www.gostarpower.com) created his own DISC assessment, which is easy for any applicant to take. First, the applicant selects where he or she falls on a *supporting versus controlling continuum;* then the person chooses where he or she falls on a *direct versus indirect continuum.* The combined result for these two categories defines which of the four personality styles the person relates to most closely—D, I, S, or C.

Supporting (Open) versus Controlling (Guarded) Do you consider yourself to be more supporting, or more controlling? Table 8.1 contains some indicators to help you distinguish between the two. After the table, mark a spot (a vertical line) on the continuum where you feel you fall.

Table 8.1

Supporting (Open)		Controlling (Guarded)	
Relaxed and warm		Formal and proper	
Opinion oriented		Fact oriented	
Supportive		Needs to have control	
Flexible about time		Time disciplined	
Relationship oriented		Keeps feelings to self	
Shares feelings easily		Task-disciplined	
Sensitive			
4	3	2	1
Very supporting	Somewhat supporting	Somewhat controlling	Very controlling

Direct versus Indirect Do you consider yourself to be more direct, or more indirect? Here are some indicators to help you distinguish between the two (Table 8.2). After the table, mark a spot (a vertical line) on the continuum where you feel you fall.

Table 8.2

Indirect	Direct
Avoids risks	Takes risks
Makes decisions slowly	Makes decisions quickly
Passive	Aggressive
Easygoing	Impatient
Listens well	Talkative
Reserved	Outgoing
Shy	Bold
Keeps opinions to self	Expresses opinions readily

A	B	C	D
Very indirect	Somewhat indirect	Somewhat direct	Very direct

Analyze the Results After the applicant completes this simple DISC assessment, transfer their marks to the grid in Figure 8.1. For example, if the person marked 2 (somewhat controlling) on the first continuum and B (somewhat indirect) on the second continuum, mark 2 and B on the grid below. Extend a line through each mark, so the two lines intersect. The quadrant in which the two lines intersect tells you the person's predominant personality type—D, I, S, or C.

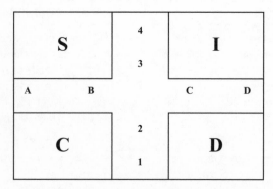

Figure 8.1   DISC Assessment Grid

Use DISC Results to Screen Applicants

As a D-personality salesperson, you may be more inclined to select an assistant who has a D- or I-personality, but that may not be the best choice. If you truly want someone who can do what you do and act as a partner, you may want someone who has a D- or I-personality, but if you are looking for an assistant to handle phone calls, fill out paperwork, file documents, and manage your schedule and accounting, you are likely to be better off choosing someone with an S- or C-personality—someone who can act in a supporting role and who doesn't want *your* job.

Interview Candidates

The skills and DISC assessments should help you screen out all but the most qualified and well-suited candidates. The next-to-final step in selecting the best person for the position is to interview the candidates. In the following sections, I offer some guidelines that can help you conduct an effective interview.

Start with General Questions

Spend some time getting to know the candidate as a person. Start with general questions that don't pertain specifically to the job at hand. If you are unaccustomed to interviewing people, here are some questions that encourage the candidate to open up:

- Are you currently employed? (If you are, why are you looking to leave your current employer?)
- What do you feel is your biggest accomplishment in life?
- What are your future goals?
- What was your worst customer service experience and how would you have handled it differently?
- Describe your best boss.
- Describe your worst boss.

Share Your Expectations

Share your goals with each candidate and describe your team's philosophy and work ethic, so the person is well aware of your expectations. Write down everything you bring to the relationship and present it to each candidate during the interview. For example, let candidates know about the type of training you provide, the opportunities for earning bonuses or commissions, the resources at your disposal, your corporate culture, and opportunities for advancement.

As you interview candidates, make sure they understand what you are looking for in terms of experience, skills and attitude. Present a detailed job description and explain what you expect. If you are willing to provide training, let the person know that although you expect him or her to ultimately be able to meet the job requirements, you will provide the necessary training and resources.

Ask the candidate how he or she feels about your expectations. Explain that finding the right match is best for both of you. If he or she accepts the position and cannot fulfill the requirements, this person is unlikely to be happy working as part of your team. Encourage the person to be honest and open—after all, honesty and openness will be required when you start working together.

Encourage the Candidate to Ask Questions

Invite the candidate to ask any questions about the position, the company, the industry, and so on. Seeing what types of questions a candidate asks provides great insight into the person's capabilities and interest in the job. It also allows you to gauge the person's communication skills and professionalism. A good candidate should always have questions prepared ahead of time; think twice about considering someone who claims to have no questions at all.

VISUAL OR VIRTUAL?

Keep in mind that assistants can be *visual* or *virtual*. A visual assistant is one who is physically present—an in-house staff member. A virtual assistant is a freelancer—a self-employed business owner who conducts business primarily over the Internet. You can use both types of assistants to increase your office productivity, but virtual assistants allow you more flexibility in scaling your workforce up or down depending on how busy you become.

Virtual assistants can do everything visual assistants do, from handling direct mailings and setting up drip e-mail campaigns to managing your e-mail and schedule, creating and managing web sites and blogs, and handling your marketing and public relations.

RETAIN YOUR BEST ASSISTANTS

Finding an outstanding assistant requires a great deal of time and effort, so do your best to keep the high-quality assistants you eventually hire. Here are some suggestions that can help you retain your best assistants:

- Hire the best people you can get, so you will remain satisfied with their performance.
- Assign meaningful job titles. Very few people like to be known as an "assistant." Create titles that convey a sense of importance, such as Sales Executive, Marketing Manager, or Director of Operations.
- Train the people you hire. As discussed in Chapter 7, you should have detailed procedure manuals.
- Equip your assistants. Provide them with the tools and resources they need to successfully complete their missions.
- Trust your assistants. Give your assistants real freedom and responsibility to make decisions. Step in only when necessary.
- Compensate assistants accordingly. Pay your assistants the going rate or better. Find other ways to reward them. Some people value status or free time to spend with their family more than money; find out what each assistant values most and reward them with it.
- Be kind to your assistants—like you, they are only human.

Ralph's Rule: If you do not have an assistant, you are one—you are your own assistant, doing much of the work that one or more assistants could be doing for you. Document everything you do, highlight the tasks you can safely delegate to others, and then hire an assistant to take on these chores.

WEEK 9

PRIORITIZE

Stephen Hopson is deaf—profoundly so, and he has been since birth. After his parents discovered this when he was three years of age, they took him to doctors who gave them a stark choice. They could enroll Stephen in a special school for the deaf that would cater to his needs throughout childhood. Or they could mainstream him in the public school system and rely on the goodwill and limited expertise of ordinary teachers to deal with students who were deaf.

Stephen's parents decided their son needed to interact with other kids who could hear, so he could learn to function in a "hearing environment." They enrolled him in public school, and their choice had a profound effect on Stephen. Sure, he suffered at the hands of a few kids who made fun of him, but more importantly, he learned how to cope as an independent kid with friends and class work and relationships.

When he got out of college, Stephen wanted to work on Wall Street. He dreamed of achieving riches as we all do. And he was no stranger to hard work. He was impeccably groomed, highly intelligent, and very motivated. But would that be enough? Stephen recalls how it took him months to convince a Merrill Lynch manager to take a chance on him. Finally, the manager did—to his great good fortune, and to Stephen's.

Within three years, Stephen's initial production had soared 1,700 percent. Competing against 12,000 financial consultants at the firm, he consistently placed in the top 1,500 in sales contests. He won trips to Bermuda, Mexico, Florida, and other resort locations. He also made Merrill Lynch's prestigious Executive Club for top sales-people three years running, overcoming his deafness to pull down $300,000 a year at Merrill Lynch.

STEPHEN'S NOT-SO-SECRET SECRET

When I got to know Stephen, I was curious as to how he went about his daily work as a stockbroker. Although I have my own systems in place for setting goals, making calls, and handling paperwork, I was curious to see if Stephen's deafness called for anything special during the course of the normal working day.

After spending some time with Stephen, I discovered that aside from the special VCO (voice carry over) telephone technology he used, Stephen pretty much went about his day just like you or me or any other top producer. (VCO technology enables a person to speak to the other party over the phone and read the person's replies on screen.) He networked. He called past customers. He asked for referrals. He wrote down his goals and planned his day around achieving them.

Perhaps most of all Stephen prioritized. How many times have you heard that you're supposed to do "first things first"? Probably a million. But how many salespeople get sidetracked every day with frivolous errands, nonproductive calls, and administrative details? Far too many. Even a top performer like me has to guard against these kinds of time-wasters. I don't always succeed entirely, but I think we concentrate better than almost anyone on tasks that are most important.

How to do this? Well, let's start by having Stephen tell us about his method at Merrill Lynch:

> The clients I approached first were always the top 20 clients that pro-duced 80 percent of my business. I called these top 20 clients almost every day to keep them informed about market conditions. They were most active in the investment decision-making process and followed my advice without the usual delaying tactics, like "Let me speak to my wife, son, daughter, lawyer, mother, father, sister, etc." It helped that they were decisive! Dealing with these kinds of clients made my job a bit easier. They were wealthy businessmen, doctors, lawyers, business

owners, socialites, etc. They were busy people, and for them time was at premium (as was mine), so we respected each others' time on the telephone. We often kept our telephone conversations quick, brief, and to the point. I rarely "chatted" with clients. Chatting was reserved for in-person appointments over breakfast, lunch, dinner, or coffee.

Once Stephen took care of his most productive clients, he would then work his way down the list of his remaining customers. "On average," he says, "all my clients heard from me at least once a month either by telephone, fax, a letter, a short note, or an e-mail. Communication was absolutely essential."

REDISCOVER YOUR A-B-Cs

Prioritizing around your top 20 clients is just one way to focus. Another salesperson I know divides his clients into A, B, and C piles. He works on the A clients first and hardest. These are the ones who produce the most business, either directly or by referrals. Only when the A list has been serviced does he turn to the B list. These are lesser prospects who with a little work might become A prospects one day. The C list is mostly the "discard pile"—those clients or deals that produce either so little profit or so much trouble that they're better off going elsewhere.

Here's another technique. Several years ago, when I first met my friend Allan Domb, the condominium king of Philadelphia, I was impressed by his ability to rank all these calls in order of importance. Allan notes what each call will be worth to him in dollars. For example, if call A succeeds, it will be worth $1,000 to him; call B might be worth $500; and call C will probably produce only $50 for him. Naturally, Allen works the A call first, then the B, and finally the C.

Simple as these techniques sound, they have been absolutely essential to the success of these salespeople. This sort of prioritizing is as basic as when your mother told you to do your homework before going out to play. You do the difficult or the important stuff first, and the rest is easy. On the other hand, if you don't take care of your most important clients first, when will you have time to catch up with them later on? Again, we all know this, but millions of salespeople, and millions more people in other walks of life, still ignore this need. Maybe we should listen to Mom more often!

DAY JOB, NIGHT JOB

There are many other useful ways of prioritizing your daily tasks. The novelist Elmore Leonard used to juggle his book writing with a daytime job at an advertising agency. He'd get up at 5 AM, work on his latest novel for a couple of hours, and then go to work at the ad agency. Eventually, he became successful enough to chuck the day job and concentrate full-time on writing novels. But while he was doing both, getting his writing done early was his way of doing the most important job first.

Whether you use an A-B-C rating, or assign a dollar amount to each task, or make a list of your 20 top clients, you'll have to develop a system. Without a system to prioritize tasks, you often waste time on less important matters.

It's also very important to know yourself. Know how you *feel* at different times of the day and use that information to assess when you are at your best. Some people are morning people, they get up early and sing with the birds, they hit the floor running, they typically make their to-do or to-call list in the evening, but they fizzle mid-afternoon. Or you may be the type who needs to have some "wake up time" to get rolling—reading the paper or creating your to-do list before you can begin talking with clients.

Whatever your preference is, don't go against the grain. Identify the time of day when you feel best, and then touch base with your clients during that time. For instance, when I focus on my real estate business, I make it a point to call each of my sellers once a week. I choose an evening the same day of the week. I have found that I am my most creative between the hours of 5 and 9 in the evening. I have to say that I didn't recognize that myself—it was my wise and attentive second in command, Lois, who figured it out, as usual!

Ralph's Rule: We salespeople face an overwhelming number of tasks each day. So do the important stuff first. It sounds simple, but you'd be surprised how many people ignore this basic advice.

KNOW YOUR PRODUCT

My wife, Kathy, and I have been settled happily for the past several years in our dream house in metropolitan Detroit. We had it built to our special wants and needs. It has many rooms and a special place for my enormous collection of electric trains. When I had the photos taken for my personal brochures, I was photographed standing in the middle of this train set. Our home is equipped with computers for us and the kids and a beautiful entertainment center where, among other things, I display my collection of special edition bottles of bourbon, including one that the folks at Jack Daniel's sent me after I wrote them a fan letter.

But here's my point. We're putting down roots now, but it wasn't always like that. During the first 20 years I spent in the real estate business, I moved about once a year. Twenty houses in 20 years. After I got married in 1985, I think I almost drove Kathy nuts with this practice. But still it was absolutely necessary for me to move a lot. It taught me what was happening in my marketplace. Nothing else could have provided such training. I got to see houses the way my customers do—as a product that I might be moving into myself.

USE YOUR PRODUCT OR SERVICE ... IF POSSIBLE

Getting to know your product and marketplace is crucial. I don't care what you sell, I'm a firm believer that you have to know your own product or services. Not just have a general understanding of it, but know it inside and out. And that means you have to experience it firsthand. If you sell Corvettes, you better drive a Corvette. If you sell guitars, you ought to play guitar.

Let me tell you about a travel agent here in metro Detroit—Patty. She was president of a company that was one of the oldest and largest trainers of travel agents in Michigan. She had also been a travel counselor herself. When I asked Patty what a good travel agent needed to do, she replied that a successful travel counselor first must be well-traveled: "You have to know the destinations, cruise ships, and resorts you will be recommending."

Patty had been to over 50 different countries and sailed on more than 15 cruise ships. With this base of experience, Patty could recommend a cruise line or a hotel or a destination to a client and talk knowledgeably about it. Not many travel counselors ever had that kind of extensive product knowledge, but it was a key element to Patty's success.

It may be easier than you think to come by your expertise. When I was moving every year, I could often reduce the sales commission because I acted as my own real estate agent. In Patty's case, she could take advantage of steep discounts offered to travel agents by airlines, hotels, and so forth. At the time, travel agents received discounts such as 75 percent off coach airfare, 50 percent off hotels, and cruises for as little as $35 a day. They were offered these discounts so they could experience these travel options firsthand.

If you're in sales and have an opportunity to be a customer as well as a salesperson, I strongly encourage you to take the opportunity. Buying and using what you sell gives you a unique perspective—your customer's perspective.

Of course, if you sell pacemakers, I don't expect you to have one implanted just so you can gain your customer's perspective. You may need to take another approach—talk extensively with patients who have pacemakers and surgeons who implant them and have to maintain them. The closer you can get to the end user of your product or service, the better.

RECRUIT REFERRALS

By the way, Patty practices another of my recommendations, which is to not be shy about passing out her business cards along the way.

"I met one of my best clients on an airplane from Miami coming back from a cruise," Patty said. "She travels a great deal and was impressed with my own travel experiences. Since that flight, based on my personal service for her, she has referred over 50 new clients to me. Similarly, I met a couple in line checking in for the same flight I was on to Manzanillo, Mexico. We chatted for a while, and I gave them a card. When we arrived home, they called me and booked a very nice Alaskan cruise and a tour to France."

Choose a product you enjoy selling. Selling requires more than just providing information; it helps to have an emotional attachment to what you sell. When you love your product, prospective customers feel the love. They quickly pick up on your enthusiasm and passion. If you aren't convinced that the product or service you're selling is the best thing since sliced bread, you're going to have a difficult time convincing someone else.

I pride myself in being a great salesperson, but just like anyone, if I discovered that the product I was selling had weaknesses that the client should know about, I wouldn't be able to get past it and would have to find the product that overcame the issues and sign up to be their salesman.

Integrity is of the utmost importance. Before you sign on to sell a product or service, ask yourself whether you would be comfortable recommending the product to your mom. This test keeps you honest.

Ralph's Rule: You can't fake product knowledge, and your customers will detect your lack of expertise. To succeed in sales, you've got to know what you are selling. The only way to do that is to experience your marketplace firsthand. Not only should you get out there and sell, but you ought to get out there and buy, too.

KNOW YOUR CLIENTS

I n Week 10, I encouraged you to know your product inside and out, but you cannot sell products or services in a vacuum. You sell products and services to the *people* who use them.

This sounds obvious, but many marketing, advertising, and sales professionals often become so obsessed with highlighting the *features* of a product or service that they completely overlook the *benefits*—all the good things the features can do for their clients.

In order to personalize the sales process, you need to demonstrate to your customers how your products and services can make their lives easier or more enjoyable or save them time and money. To accomplish this well, you need to know your clients and how they typically use the products and services you sell. In this chapter, I show you how to develop a better knowledge of your clients.

WHO'S REALLY YOUR CLIENT?

A top hair salon owner asked me to help him identify and capitalize on new revenue-generating opportunities. He was thinking I would give him some advice on products and services to offer patrons. Instead, I began by asking him who he thought were his best clients.

He singled out his regulars—the people who scheduled monthly or weekly appointments, showed up on time, rarely complained, and delivered referral business.

I disagreed. I told him to look at it a different way. His clients were actually the people on the floor who booked business—his hair stylists, manicurists, and massage therapists. Instead of focusing on pleasing the people who walked through the doors for a manicure, massage, or wash and cut, he needed to focus on pleasing the hair stylists, manicurists, and massage therapists. They needed to be happy and growing in knowledge in order to properly service their clients' needs.

Before you begin studying your clients, take some time to identify the people who are really your clients—you might be surprised at who they really are.

USE WHAT YOU SELL

You can get to know your products and services by using them yourself. Becoming a consumer of your own products and services is a great way to get to know your customers, as well.

If you sell a particular make and model of car, drive it yourself to discover firsthand every feature of the car and how each feature benefits you. If you sell camping gear, go camping and use the products you sell to determine how they can make your campouts safer and more enjoyable. Regardless of what you sell—racing bicycles, snowboards, computers, clothing, furniture, you name it—you will do a better job of selling it if you use it yourself.

PARTICIPATE IN CONSUMER COMMUNITIES

Consumers often congregate on the Internet or in local communities to share their enthusiasm and knowledge of certain products and services. You can find communities for people who own VW Beetles, athletes who play any number of sports, patients who share information on medications used to treat specific illnesses, web sites where people gather to learn more about buying and selling a home, and much more.

These communities are tremendous resources where salespeople can learn more about the clients they serve. Clients who become involved in these groups often ask the same questions that your clients will ask or at least think about asking. They share the same problems. They seek out the same information.

By becoming involved in these communities, you can develop an intimate knowledge of your clients and learn how to serve them more effectively. In addition, if you succeed in establishing yourself as a trusted expert in these communities, you begin to develop relationships that sell.

CONSULT WITH OTHER DEPARTMENTS

Sales reps often become isolated from the other departments in their companies, including customer service, technical support, and product development, but people in these departments are often excellent resources for getting to know your clients—what they need, what they want, the questions they most commonly ask, and the most common issues they encounter.

As a salesperson, you should be making the rounds at your company to gather as much information about your customers as possible. Schedule monthly meetings with managers from other departments, especially those departments that communicate directly with clients, so you can share information. By sharing information, you can all work together to improve all aspects of your products and services, your delivery, and the way you serve customers after the sale. Through your combined efforts, you improve customer satisfaction, which drives more sales.

LEARN YOUR CUSTOMER'S BUSINESS

If you are in business-to-business sales, your clients' business success is your success. The more profitable your clients become, the more products and services they can afford to buy from you. Find out what your clients need to succeed, which usually includes the following:

- *Products:* If you do not carry the products your customer needs to be successful, either add them to your product line or team up with someone who carries the product. You may be able to trade referrals with suppliers who offer different products.

- *Services:* If you do not offer the services your customer needs to be successful and you know a company that does, contact the company and work out a deal to refer clients to one another or perhaps negotiate a referral fee with that company.
- *Information:* You can often win clients by supplying them with the information they need via your web site, blog, or newsletter.
- *Training:* Consider providing training (either free or for a fee), instructing your clients on how to make better use of the products and services you sell or how to become more profitable.
- *Financing:* Many small-business owners require financing to get up and running. By offering them financing to purchase your products and services, you can often make a sale and win a client for life.
- *Personnel:* Skilled and talented individuals keep businesses running and growing. If a lack of qualified personnel is getting in the way of your client's success, you may be able to recommend qualified candidates.

GATHER FEEDBACK FROM CLIENTS

One of the best ways to discover more about your clients is to ask them to provide feedback on everything from the products and services you sell to your customer service. Consider distributing a survey or questionnaire to your best clients. To increase the number of people who respond, do the following:

- Keep the survey or questionnaire brief.
- Include a postage-paid envelope for returning feedback.
- Offer a discount or free gift to everyone who returns a completed questionnaire.

When you begin receiving completed surveys or questionnaires, have your assistant input the data into a spreadsheet or database, so you can tally and analyze the results.

You may also want to ask for feedback via your web site or blog. Include a form that customers can fill out to e-mail you questions, suggestions, or complaints.

Ralph's Rule: One of your main goals as a salesperson should be to make your clients as successful as possible. Whether you are trying to put a family into the right vehicle or home, provide physicians with prescription medications that most effectively treat their patients, or supply businesses with the products and services they need to serve their customers, the more successful you can make them, the more successful you will become.

WEEK 12

RECOGNIZE THE DIFFERENCE BETWEEN CUSTOMERS AND CLIENTS

To most salespeople, the terms *customer* and *client* are synonymous; they both purchase products and services. However, I like to draw more of a distinction between the two. I think *customers* buy products and services from *order takers.* Customers know what they want and where to get it, and simply place an order.

The people who serve customers are not salespeople; they're order takers. They are not responsible for marketing, advertising, selling, or helping their customers make wise purchase decisions. The closest they come to customer service is when they hand the product to the customer and collect the money.

Salespeople, like attorneys, have clients who depend on them for their expertise and guidance. Clients do not always know what they want or where to get it. They may not know how to get the most out of the products or services they purchase. They rely on knowledgeable salespeople to assist them in identifying their needs and selecting the products and services that can best meet those needs.

BE A SALESPERSON, NOT AN ORDER TAKER

Order takers do nothing to *build their business*. They merely *do business*. They rely on their company to deliver high-quality leads, and then they make the sale. On the other hand, salespeople are constantly shaking the bushes to generate their own leads. They call everyone they know, ask for referrals, and shamelessly self-promote to draw more clients and increase sales and revenue. Salespeople are proactive, whereas order takers are reactive. While order takers make excuses, salespeople make sales.

To achieve success, be a salesperson, not an order taker. Never wait around for your sales manager to tell you what to do, for business to "pick up," or for somebody else to provide the leads or resources you need to achieve your goals. Take the initiative, develop an entrepreneurial mindset, and act as eager as a small-business owner to make your mini-business a resounding success.

CUSTOMER SERVICE IS KEY

Order takers often worry about their bottom line—revenue, profits, and commissions. Salespeople focus on the top line—their clients. As a salesperson, serving your customers becomes your number-one priority. People become more important than profit. Attend to the people (your top line), and you never have to worry about profits (your bottom line).

When I talk about customer service, I am not only talking about serving your clients in a professional capacity. Take a sincere interest in the lives of your clients, and if you can help them achieve their personal goals as well as their professional goals, you can often build business as well.

BECOME A PROBLEM SOLVER

In addition to being a top-notch customer service rep, a good salesperson solves problems. In my business, real estate, one of the biggest problems my clients face is coming up with enough money for a down payment.

Faced with a customer who really can't afford their product, order takers will do one of two things: They'll either turn the customer away or sell them the product anyway without regard for their financial well-being. Both approaches are wrong. By turning away prospective clients, you lose not only their business but any additional referral business they may have sent your way in the future. If you proceed with the sale anyway without concern for their financial well-being, you make one sale at the cost of future sales and referrals. Either way, you both lose.

Spend some time getting to know prospective clients. Assist them in analyzing the challenges they face and developing creative solutions. In my business, for example, when a couple is convinced they cannot afford to purchase a home, I can refer them to any number of reliable and trustworthy mortgage brokers who can make their dream a reality. In my foreclosure business, I often assist homeowners who are facing foreclosure keep their homes. In many cases, I lose out on potentially lucrative investment properties, but in the long run, doing the right thing pays off. People I have helped often direct my attention to even better deals later on.

Zig Ziglar is famous for saying that if you help everyone around you get what they want, you will ultimately get what you want. Follow his lead. Solve your clients' problems, and you are likely to discover that your own problems magically disappear.

Ralph's Rule: A salesperson who works only on the easy deals is nothing more than an order taker. A real salesperson is one who makes something good happen when the client's well-being is on the line.

WEEK 13

UNDER-PROMISE, OVER-DELIVER

What's the difference between Disney World and an ordinary amusement park? Expectations. The actual rides and attractions may not be very different, but Disney consistently exceeds its visitors' expectations. Disney provides a total family entertainment, not just a ride here and a ride there. It's Disney's ability to go beyond what vacationers expect that has made Disney World one of the most famous vacation destinations.

We can learn from Disney World's experience. Achieving a successful sale is largely a matter of exceeding customer expectations. Notice I don't say that closing a transaction by itself is enough to qualify a deal as successful. It's not. Remember, we're trying to set up long-term relationships with customers, not tag them for one-time commissions. Your customers of today will be back tomorrow only if you exceed what they expected.

How to do that? Well, over time you'll get a better feel for your marketplace and for what customers expect. But until you can go merely by instinct, here are a few rules I've found helpful for exceeding expectations.

ASK!

A salesperson should be asking questions all the time. You'll want to know who's going to be using the product and under what conditions. If you work in a camping supply store, for example, and a client is in the market for a sleeping bag, you'll need to find out who's going to be sleeping in that bag. Is the person buying the sleeping bag going to be using it or is it a gift for a child or teenager? Is the person who will be using the bag going to be sleeping in subzero temperatures? Will the person need to carry the bag long distances (in which case, the person will need something fairly light and compact)?

Remember, the word "ask" consist of three letters: A is for "ask"; S is for ask "simply" rather than in complicated or overly clever ways; and K is for "keep on asking."

UNCOVER SOFT EXPECTATIONS

Customers usually have both obvious expectations about a product or service and hidden, or soft, expectations. A car buyer may tell the salesperson she expects to pay $20,000 and get a car with air conditioning and antilock brakes, but the unspoken demand may have more to do with expectations of long-term reliability. Many car buyers expect not to have any serious trouble with a new car for five years minimum. A salesperson who's used to selling on points like style and engine power may be mystified when a customer leaves for another dealership. But product reliability is one of those soft expectations that become crucial to making a connection with your client.

Often a client isn't even aware of these soft expectations. Suppose you sell photocopy machines that can collate and staple and copy in both color and black and white; but again there may be expectations that are even more important. Simplicity may be a concern; the client may want everyone in his office to be able to use the machine so he doesn't have to dedicate a separate employee to copying duties. Or he may expect the seller to provide free training and on-site, same-day service in case of a breakdown. These are the soft expectations that often do not come out in typical sales calls. But these are the ones that will make or break the long-term relationship.

How do you find out about these soft expectations? By asking questions. Spend more time talking with a customer up front (actually listening more than talking), so you can uncover the soft expectations. This can help you decide a more effective way to present your products and services.

FOLLOW UP

You should always call your customers shortly after they've taken delivery. Even though product quality has improved over the years, some bad products still get shipped. It's up to us to make sure our customers are happy with what we've sold them. Ask whether it's working okay, whether the delivery staff was helpful, and whether there's anything else you and your company can do. If there's even a hint of trouble, you've got some more work to do trying to straighten things out.

THINK TOTAL SERVICE

Put yourself in your customers' shoes. What they expect from a product is that it will work as advertised and that you as the salesperson will stand behind it. But you can exceed their expectations by giving them even more. For example, my all-time favorite products are my digital audio recorders.

I actually have two of them. I keep one recorder with me so I can dictate memos to my staff night and day. I then leave the recorder with one of my assistants to type the memos and distribute them to the appropriate team members via e-mail. I take the other one with me to record new memos and notes.

The thing I like most about my digital audio recorders is the company that sells them to me. I travel a lot, so these recorders really take a beating, but I need them to function properly 24/7. My supplier knows this and offers an extended warranty complete with technical support and service. If I roll over one of these recorders with my truck, I can get a replacement in a matter of hours rather than days.

That's the sort of spirit you need to create for customers. And you do that by learning what customers expect and then giving them more.

Ralph's Rule: Many salespeople try to "manage" expectations, but that's a mistake. You can't control customers' thoughts. Simply find out what they want and need. Then give them something over and above that. Pay particular attention to the softer or service side of the transaction.

WEEK 14

LEVERAGE THE POWER OF YOUR DISABILITIES

I carry an official diagnosis of Attention Deficit Hyper-activity Disorder (ADHD). I am afraid that if I receive treatment for it, I will no longer be as energetic and creative as I am. In some ways, this disability of mine is a real handicap. In a single day, I might come up with a half dozen great ideas. I get everyone around me excited about these ideas and involved in bringing them to fruition. The next day, I wake up with another half dozen ideas that are even better, and I am determined to get rolling on these ideas, too. I am constantly shifting gears and direction and overloading and overwhelming everyone around me. Need-less to say, I go through a lot of staff members, partners, and other people who help me achieve my dreams. This is the downside of my ADHD.

The upside is that I am highly energetic and can process loads of data. I can sit in on a meeting and be completely aware of everything everyone says while I am reading and responding to e-mail mes-sages, catching up on my Google News alerts, or reviewing chapters for a book I am working on. Multitasking for me is no challenge—it is a way of life.

I have also discovered that I can achieve a higher retention rate if I listen to audio recordings played back at double the speed. In other words, I can listen to a two-hour audio book in an hour and remember the information longer than if I took the full two hours to listen to it. I mentioned this to my doctor who is now researching this phenomenon to determine whether it can help his other patients.

IDENTIFY YOUR ABILITIES AND DISABILITIES

According to Socrates, "The unexamined life is not worth living." This is true both in your personal and professional life. To make full use of all of your skills and talents, you need to know what you are good at and what you are not so good at.

I know that I am a lousy manager. I drive people so hard that I often drive them right out the door. I have absolutely no idea of how to schedule projects or pace myself. To compensate, I have a second in command, Lois Maljak, who tries her best to rein me in. She acts as a buffer between me and the people around me who are responsible for executing the thousands of ideas I have over the course of any given year.

Grab a pad of paper and create a two-column list. In the left column, jot down all the things you are really good at—talking to people, coming up with ideas, managing people, talking on the phone, planning, and so on. In the column on the right, list all of what you consider to be your disabilities. Perhaps you are not so good at delegating tasks, telling people what a great job they have done, or mastering new technologies. Maybe you tend to be impatient with people. Whatever your abilities or disabilities are, write them down, and be honest about it.

I received my official diagnosis of ADHD just prior to my 48th birthday. One of my assistants mentioned her concerns to a client of mine who happens to specialize in this field. My client replied that in order to gain a professional opinion, she would need to perform a series of tests, but based on her experience, she would say that "it is as clear as the nose on your face." After performing her diagnostic tests, she concluded that I did, indeed, have ADHD.

IDENTIFY THE POSITIVE IN YOUR DISABILITIES

Every ability and disability has a flip side. I have known people with high IQs who have turned their innate intelligence into a handicap.

They think they are so smart, they never have to work at anything. They get lazy and careless. I also know people who have what most "normal" people would consider a severe handicap use their "disability" to improve their lives and the lives of everyone around them.

Kyle Maynard—born with his arms ending at his elbows and his legs ending at his knees—managed to become a Georgia state high school wrestling champion, motivational speaker, and author of *No Excuses: The True Story of a Congenital Amputee Who Became a Champion in Wrestling and in Life* (2006, Regnery Publishing). Some may claim that Maynard was able to overcome or compensate for his disability, but I like to think that part of his success is due to this disability and how he, his parents, his coaches, and others responded to it. Life raised the bar, and Kyle seized the challenge.

One of the most inspirational people I know is Stephen Hopson, whom you met in Chapter 9. Even though Stephen has been deaf since birth, he has excelled in school, in his career, and throughout his life transforming his own misfortune into what many would consider a fortune (not only in terms of wealth and possessions, but in what really matters most—human relationships).

According to Stephen, "After a few years, I was making more money that I had ever thought I could, but I was experiencing a burning desire to do more. So at the end of 1996, I left my six-figure, award-winning career at Merrill Lynch to become a motivational speaker and author."

The first book Stephen wrote was *Chicken Soup for the College Soul*. Since then, Stephen has authored two more books: *Heartwarmers* and *True Spiritual Adventures from Around the World*, and he continues to motivate people around the world. To find out more about Stephen, visit his web site at www.sjhopson.com.

Ralph's Rule: Success is not a matter of brains or beauty but of desire and hard work. Make the most of your abilities, but don't overlook the untapped or underutilized potential of your disabilities.

WEEK 15

TURN PROBLEMS INTO OPPORTUNITIES

I know professionals who have banned the word "problem" from their businesses and demand that all team members use the word "challenge" in its place. I believe this is a bit severe. I have no issues with the word "problem," because to me every problem reveals opportunities for inventions, partnerships, and new business.

Realize that every single invention came about because of the need to solve some problem. Someone invented the wheel to drag objects more easily from one place to another. Someone invented the umbrella to keep from getting wet or to provide shade where sunshine was plentiful but trees were not. When people became tired of wrestling with their clothes to dress and undress, they invented buttons, zippers, snaps, hooks, and Velcro.

LOOK FOR TROUBLE

You've probably heard the saying that goes, "That guy's just looking for trouble." We all know that stirring up trouble is counterproductive, but looking for trouble can actually be a good thing. By identifying problems, you can discover lucrative business opportunities, so keep your eyes and ears open.

Some of my most innovative ideas have developed out of problems I faced. I was one of the first real estate agents in the country to implement a team-based approach to selling real estate. I knew I had a problem—I hated answering phones, taking messages, and filling out paperwork—so I decided to solve the problem by hiring and training assistants to handle these tasks for me. As a result, I not only grew my business through team-building, but I was also able to parlay my good fortune into speaking engagements, coaching sessions, and book deals. I recently co-authored a book on teams with RISMedia founder and CEO John Featherston, titled *Power Teams: The Complete Guide to Building and Managing a Winning Real Estate Agent Team.*

When I set my goal to sell 300 homes in a year, I had a problem—I could not possibly show homes to enough couples to sell that many in a year. To solve the problem, I started driving two, three, and four couples around at a time to show them homes. I could quadruple my production simply by purchasing a larger vehicle and having assistants handle the increased paperwork.

I am not a skilled writer. As someone who wants to write books, that's a problem, so I have partnered with professional writers to co-author nearly a dozen books.

Recently, I became involved with a company called Face to Face Live (www.f2fl.com) that specializes in providing high-quality videoconferencing systems. Videoconferencing has been around since the 1960s but never really has taken off; it never has received what I would consider *The Jetsons* status. Recently, however, the popularity of videoconferencing has begun to boom. Part of this is due to the fact that the technology is much better and more affordable, but I think that the growing popularity of videoconferencing is primarily due to problems. With airline travel becoming more costly, more complicated, and riskier, companies can save loads of money and increase production by videoconferencing rather than having personnel fly back and forth.

BECOME A PROBLEM SOLVER

Most of your clients have problems. This is why they need you. As a salesperson, you are primarily a problem solver, so listen carefully when your clients begin to complain about something—you might just hear about a new golden opportunity.

If you sell cars and a client shows up complaining that the SUV she is driving is a gas hog, you have just identified the client's problem and have a golden opportunity to sell her a brand new vehicle that is stingy on gas.

If you are a real estate agent and hear a couple complaining of having too little room for their growing family, you have just identified the client's problem and have a golden opportunity to sell them a larger home (as well as listing their home for them).

If you discover that you are turning away prospective clients because they simply cannot afford your products and services, they have a problem you can solve. Look into providing the clients with financing. In addition to making your products more affordable, a finance department can become another source of revenue for you.

Take a lesson from Best Buy. The company was selling gobs of computers and software, but many of its clients were having trouble keeping their systems up and running, connecting to the Internet, and networking two or more computers. Best Buy recognized these problems and launched its Geek Squad—a new revenue generator that does house calls to provide onsite technical support and service. In addition to generating more revenue for the company through fees for service calls, the Geek Squad also boosts sales of computer gear, software, and accessories and advertises Best Buy through its fleet of distinctive VW Beetles.

LOOK FOR PROBLEMS IN YOUR OWN BUSINESS, TOO

In addition to assisting your clients in solving their problems, keep a close watch for trouble in your own business. Listen to other sales reps in your office, other people in your company, your assistants, and other team members. These folks are often closer to problems than you are and can tell you about times when they themselves or the company's clients have encountered problems.

If you notice a problem in your company, other companies that are similar to yours are probably experiencing the same problem. This could be a revenue-generating opportunity that enables you to charge other companies a fee for solving this problem for them or an opportunity to establish goodwill in your business community by sharing your solution to the problem.

Ralph's Rule: Look at problems as opportunities, and you will have a never-ending supply of opportunities. If you can invent a solution to an age-old problem, you place yourself in a unique position to corner the market.

BRAND YOURSELF: YOU, INC.

C lose your eyes and imagine the president of the United States or Madonna or Martin Luther King Jr. You can probably come up with a pretty clear image of what they look like because these people have attained celebrity or even legendary status. This is what you want, too, and proper branding can deliver it, but first, you need a central brand focus—something unique that is totally you, something that will excite you and everyone around you.

A real estate colleague of mine in Montgomery, Alabama, Sandra Nickel, is known far and wide as "The Hat Lady." She wears a distinctive hat wherever she goes. Her hat logo appears on her business card, on all of her correspondence, and even on her web site "Invest in Montgomery, Alabama" (www.investinmontgomeryalabama .com). Sandra has a solid team of real estate professionals who handle the daily business. She functions as the rainmaker, ensuring that the phones keep ringing and the Internet remains abuzz with the voices of interested buyers and sellers. She tells the story of Midtown Montgomery and volunteers tirelessly to improve the community. In the process, the Hat Lady attracts a lot of attention . . . and lots of business.

This is what branding is all about, and when you do it right, your brand becomes synonymous with the products and services you sell—just like Kleenex is to tissues.

NAILING DOWN MY BRAND

Several years ago, I decided to form a brand around an 11-foot-tall, 500-pound nail. The nail already had some local appeal and a good story behind it. I purchased it on eBay for $3,000 (the seller donated the proceeds to a local charity), and then I proceeded to parade it around town and loan it out for charity events. Now, all of my marketing materials have the BigNail on them. I even have a web site about it at (you've probably guessed) BigNail.com, where you can read all about it. (BigNail.com is the site to go for more information on branding.)

I am not suggesting that you have your own 11-foot, 500-pound nail custom built for you, but you should have something that sets you apart from the competition and will appeal to your target market. Then, you should drive home that image in every piece of your marketing materials, including your web sites and blogs.

ASSEMBLE A MARKETING PACKET

To establish a brand presence, the first thing you will need is an attractive marketing packet that you can deliver to prospects before meeting with them. You should have a standard packet for prospective clients and put together custom marketing packets to introduce yourself to reporters, potential partners, and other professionals you may want to team up with. Your marketing materials should all include the following:

- Your name.
- Your photo.
- Your logo or company logo.
- Complete contact information (phone and fax numbers, e-mail address, mailing address, and so on).
- Web site and blog addresses.

If you are artistic, you can design the marketing materials yourself and take them over to a local print shop to have them produced in quantity. Otherwise, hire a graphic artist to draw up some designs from which to choose. The proprietor of the print shop can recommend local artists, or a colleague may refer you to one. Try to find someone who can design everything for you, including your web site or blog when you are ready to add those components to your marketing campaign.

Your marketing packet should include the following materials:

- *Folder:* A legal-size folder into which you can place all of your other marketing materials. Since the folder is the first item that prospects will see, make sure it has an impeccable design.

- *Business card:* Your business card is a key component of your marketing packet, and you will also hand it out to everyone you meet, even if they are not receiving the full packet. Don't try to trim corners. Use high-quality card stock with raised lettering. Your business card should include your logo, a photo of you, your job title or a brief mention of what you do, your phone number, e-mail address, and main web site address.

- *Letter of introduction:* A one- or two-page letter introducing yourself and describing some of your major accomplishments and your commitment to clients can help prospects get to know you better.

- *Resume or curriculum vitae:* Your resume or curriculum vitae should highlight your knowledge, education, certifications, areas of expertise, experience, professional associations, community service, and other items that establish your credibility and expertise. (If you choose to do something more extensive, consider creating your own unique selling proposition or USP. You can check out my USP at www.aboutralph.com/about_ralph/ ralph_roberts_unique_selling_proposition.html.)

- *Statement of benefits:* Why should this prospect hire you rather than one of your competitors? What can you offer the client that others in the field cannot? Put down in writing a list of key ways the person will benefit by choosing you.

- *Testimonials:* Prospects generally place more trust in what other people say about you than what you say about yourself. Whenever a client thanks you for a job well done, you should ask for two things—referrals to friends and family and a testimonial that you can quote in your marketing materials. Use these testimonials in your marketing packet.

- *Press clippings:* When a newspaper or magazine prints a story about you, they can usually provide you with reprints of the article, so you do not have to purchase stacks of the magazine or newspaper. Always order reprints and include them in your marketing packet. Positive press reinforces the message that you are a credible authority who delivers on promises.

Once you have a logo and brand identity, you are prepared to start spreading the word about your brand and establishing a brand presence through shameless self-promotion, as discussed in Week 17.

Ralph's Rule: Consistency is critical in branding. Everything should have a consistent appearance and color scheme. Creative people tend to want to add some variation because they are afraid of coming across as boringly consistent, but this is a common mistake. Consistency tattoos your image on the minds of your clients, prospects, competitors, and others in the industry. It gives you a recognizable face.

WEEK 17

ENGAGE IN SHAMELESS SELF-PROMOTION

M any salespeople are in a constant hunt for business, which is certainly okay, but rather than look for targets, I prefer to become a target myself, and I do it through shameless self-promotion.

Due to my marketing efforts, I am constantly approached by prospective clients who want me to buy or sell their home, local and national news organizations who need insights and information for real estate related stories, companies who want me to be their spokesperson, sales professionals who need mentoring or coaching, publishers who want me to write books, and organizations from around the world who want me to speak to their members. I can cherry-pick the opportunities I want to pursue. I wake up every day knowing that I will never be without a lucrative opportunity.

In this chapter, I highlight the key areas you need to focus on when launching your own shameless self-promotional campaign.

FOCUS ON *SELF-*PROMOTION

Before clients will buy *from* you, they have to buy *into* you. They have to know you and trust you, know what you sell, and believe that you are going to treat them fairly and with respect. The goal of your marketing campaign should always be to build a high positive profile that constantly reinforces your image and the fact that you are knowledgeable and trustworthy in the minds of your clients and prospective clients.

You may also be marketing your company and the products and services you sell, but those entities are only peripheral interests. By promoting your *self,* you ensure long-term success. Even if you change companies or start selling other products, you retain all the benefits of the time, money, and energy you invested in your self-promotional efforts.

Caution: Although your marketing campaign needs to focus on you, I am not recommending that you use this opportunity to take an ego trip. The real focus is not solely on you but what you can do for your clients.

MAKE IT A PRIORITY

Far too many people approach self-promotion as something they do when they have time. They run a TV commercial and see how that does. The next week, they place an ad in the paper or run something on the radio to determine whether that will draw more business. Perhaps they dabble on the Internet, creating a second-rate web site that they later lose interest in.

These hit-or-miss marketing campaigns are destined to fail, because they have no lasting impact on clients and prospects whose minds are infiltrated with a daily barrage of advertisements. A single ad does not imprint an image on the collective mind of your audience.

To be effective, a marketing campaign must be comprehensive (as in multimedia) and unrelenting (as in never let up). You need to build a marketing blitz that never loses its intensity. Eventually, your marketing will develop a life of its own—it will "go viral," delivering countless opportunities to your door.

START ON THE INTERNET

One of the first and best places to begin any marketing campaign is on the Internet because the Internet is the first place your clients will go when they have a problem or need information about products and services. They may not order your products or services on the Internet, but I can almost guarantee that they will shop on the Internet.

In addition, the Internet is one of the most affordable venues for marketing and advertising whatever you sell. For less than a hundred dollars a year, you can set up your own blog, complete with a unique address, such as www.YourName.com. This can become the focal point of your marketing campaign, giving you a central location where clients and prospective clients can find you and then find out more about you.

By establishing a presence on the Internet and building a reputation as the go-to guy or gal for the products and services you sell, you position yourself to become the sales representative of choice when someone is finally prepared to make a purchase.

To establish a strong Internet presence, focus on the following four areas:

- *Blog:* Blogging provides a quick and easy way to establish yourself on the Web. Posting content is as easy as filling out a form. For details about adding a blogging component to your self-promotional and marketing campaigns, refer to Week 37, "Launch Your Own Blog."

- *Web site:* A web site is like a blog without weekly updates. It consists primarily of static pages and tends to be more difficult to create and maintain. However, newer content management system (CMS) tools are available to make web sites almost as easy as blogs to create and maintain.

- *Newsletter:* Publishing a weekly or monthly newsletter is a great way to stay in touch with clients and appeal to new, prospective clients. Make sure you add a page to your site where people can register to subscribe to receive your newsletter via e-mail. This enables you to capture e-mail addresses, which come in very handy for any future marketing campaigns.

- *Social merchandising:* Consumers often hesitate to make a purchase because they are waiting for permission from their peers.

With social merchandising, you can nurture a community of consumers who eagerly promote you and whatever you sell. Some of the most popular places to conduct social merchandising are on social networking sites, such as MySpace.com and FaceBook.

Launching a web site or blog is no guarantee that people from around the country or around the world will flock to it. If you create a blog and post a great deal of unique content that is in high demand, search engines, including Google, will index your content, and you will soon have plenty of visitors. Otherwise, you will need to use other elements of your campaign to help drive traffic to your sites.

DISTRIBUTE REGULAR PRESS RELEASES

You may get "discovered" simply by posting content to your blog, distributing your newsletter, doing good deeds in your community, or writing articles for other publications, but the media probably will not go looking for you. They may need a little help, and you can often assist them in discovering you by distributing regular press releases.

When a newsworthy event occurs (or is about to occur), start writing. Announcing something that happened a week ago is not news. As you write, follow these guidelines for composing your press release:

- *Read some sample press releases first.* Model your press release after others that you find interesting and informative.
- *Start with an intriguing headline.* Nobody is going to read your press release if the headline sounds boring. The headline should draw people into the article.
- *Start the first paragraph with the city, state, and date.* Location and time set the stage for the rest of what you have to say.
- *Stick to a single page.* You have very little time to make your point. Remember, your goal is to convince people who read the release to call you. Limiting your press release to between 300 and 750 words is best.
- *Don't advertise.* A press release is an announcement worthy of the news, not an advertisement for products or services.

- *Edit carefully.* Your press release is a reflection of you, so make sure it is well-written and free of typos and grammatical errors.

- *Obtain permissions for quoted material.* If you want to quote some-one in a press release, obtain permission from the person or company you're quoting.

- *Include contact information.* You want the press calling or e-mailing you or your assistant to set up interviews and perhaps appearances.

Several companies can assist you in distributing your press release, including PRWeb at www.prwebdirect.com, 24/7 Press Release at www.24/7pressrelease.com, and RISMedia (real estate-related press releases) at www.rismedia.com. You can search the Web for "press release distribution" or other related words and phrases to find a hundred other such companies, or e-mail me at RalphRoberts@RalphRoberts.com, and I can recommend a few more options.

DRAW FREE PUBLICITY AND POSITIVE PRESS

A close friend and colleague of mine, Michael Soon Lee, founder of EthnoConnect (www.EthnoConnect.com), specializes in cross-cultural selling. We are co-authoring *Cross-Cultural Selling For Dum-mies.* He relates the following story of how he drew some valuable free publicity and positive PR simply by doing the right thing for a local high school:

> When I was Chairman of the Board of a credit union in the San Francisco Bay Area, thieves broke into a local high school softball team's locker room and stole all of their uniforms and equipment for the upcoming season. We jumped into action and allocated $5,000 from our marketing budget to replace everything they had lost. The coach and school prin-cipal were so appreciative that they called the local media. When we presented them with the check, almost every local radio and television station along with many of the area newspapers ran the story.
>
> One advertising agency estimated that our investment netted us over $30,000 worth of publicity. That's not the reason we donated the funds, but the publicity we received was certainly a pleasant, unexpected surprise.

Although you can spend hundreds of thousands of dollars on professionally produced multimedia marketing campaigns, you can also generate a great deal of free publicity and positive press by investing only your time and expertise:

- *Contact local reporters and journalists.* Reporters and journalists need to crank out a steady stream of stories, and they are always in need of industry experts. Let them know who you are and what you do. Most of these folks are on tight deadlines, so be sure you're available at a moment's notice and train yourself to talk in short, significant sound bites.

- *Get involved in high-profile community activities.* Demonstrate your commitment to the communities you serve by giving back to the people who keep you in business. Communities can be online communities (such as user groups), medical communities (if you sell pharmaceuticals or medical equipment), neighborhoods, local business organizations, and so on.

- *Take on leadership roles.* Join community-based organizations and take on leadership roles to raise your profile. Leaders may not know all members, but all members usually know who the leaders are.

INVEST IN PAID ADVERTISING

Most of the advertising media I discuss in this chapter is free or very inexpensive, but you also have the option to invest in paid advertising. If potential clients watch TV, listen to the radio, or read the local newspaper, you should establish a presence in these media channels. Following are some options to consider:

- *TV commercial:* Hire a local video production company to produce a 30-second commercial for you and pay for a spot on one or more stations that your clients are likely to watch.

- *Radio advertisement:* Radio advertising has lost some of its effectiveness because fewer and fewer people tune in, but if you know of a hugely popular radio station that many of your clients are likely to listen to, give it a shot.

- *Newspaper advertisement:* If you sell products locally to general consumers, consider placing an ad in a local newspaper. Ask the sales rep at the newspaper about *remnant ad* opportunities;

newspapers often offer left-over advertising space at bargain rates.

- *Billboard:* Another good way to advertise locally is to purchase some advertising space on a billboard in an area with lots of traffic. Keep in mind, however, that drivers have very little time to read anything you place on the billboard. Use an attractive design that includes your photo and contact information, and keep your message short.

- *Internet advertising:* Most of the big search engines offer pay-per-click (PPC) advertising, displaying ads on their own site and on partner sites for products and services. Rates vary depending on how much you are willing to pay to have a higher ad placement on the site. You pay only if someone clicks the ad. For more about PPC advertising, visit Google Adwords at adwords.google.com and Yahoo! Search Marketing at search marketing.yahoo.com.

Ralph's Rule: Don't let up. Maintaining an unrelenting marketing campaign means doing something every day to promote yourself—writing a press release, talking to a reporter, posting something on the Web, showing up for a community meeting. This takes a good deal of energy. Most people give up long before their campaign starts to show results. Keep at it.

WEEK 18

SEE BUSINESS WHERE IT ISN'T

I f you are like most people, you have probably heard of at least a few inventors who have earned fortunes on what appear to be obvious ideas. A case in point is the Breathe Right Strip invented by chronic sinus sufferer Bruce Johnson. What could be more obvious than a device that holds your nostrils open from the outside to help you breathe?

Coming up with inventions and other innovative ideas is more challenging than it appears because they often develop in a vacuum. Before these gadgets and schemes exist, someone with an imagination needs to envision them or "pull them out of thin air."

The same is true in business. With hindsight's 20/20 vision, we can easily see good ideas where business already exists. One look at Starbucks coffee shops, and we immediately realize what a great idea it is to have a high-class, high-quality coffee shop where patrons always feel welcome to work, relax, and meet friends and colleagues. Before Starbucks, however, nobody really envisioned such a place existing globally. It took somebody who could see business where it isn't.

IDENTIFY UNSERVED AND UNDERSERVED MARKETS

One way to see business where it isn't is to look for markets that you and your competitors are not serving or fully serving. Say you are selling videoconferencing systems. Businesses and schools would probably be your most obvious clients. They have both the need and the money for these high-tech systems and can probably save enough on travel to more than cover the cost.

You and your competitors will aggressively pursue these markets, but to gain a competitive edge, you would do well to see business where it isn't. Who could really make use of videoconferencing that neither you nor your competition is currently pursuing? These other potential markets may include the following:

- *Courts of law and attorneys:* Legal matters often get delayed simply because gathering all involved parties is such a hassle. Courts and attorneys could use videoconferencing to take depositions, review evidence and documents, and even hold a trial.
- *Government agencies:* Government agencies often have a difficult time serving outlying areas. Through videoconferencing, they could affordably extend their reach.
- *Health care providers:* Some of the top medical specialists may be in another state or country. With videoconferencing, physicians could consult with patients and with one another regardless of their physical location.
- *Financial services:* Financial analysts and advisors often meet with clients to review their financial plans and portfolios. With videoconferencing, nobody has to travel out of their way to attend a meeting.
- *Energy—oil and gas:* Oil and gas fields are often in remote locations. While experts must often travel to these fields, executives may not have to be physically present to know what is going on. Videoconferencing can also be used to monitor operations from remote locations.
- *Engineering and construction:* Large construction projects often require the collaborative efforts of engineers, contractors, and subcontractors. With videoconferencing, experts can gather in a virtual conference room to consult as a group.

- *Retailers:* Large retail chains spend a great deal of time and travel to make their stores consistent and convey corporate expectations. Videoconferencing can significantly improve communications throughout these organizations.

- *Human resources (all sectors):* Human resource (HR) departments are in charge of recruiting, screening, and hiring new applicants; managing benefits programs; and ensuring compliance. Rather than running themselves ragged trying to stay in touch with everyone, they can use videoconferencing to host meetings via virtual conference rooms.

Unserved and underserved markets can also consist of groups of people that you and your competition have ignored in the past—certain generations, such as teenagers or retirees; racial or ethnic groups; the opposite sex; and so on.

Customers from other cultures represent a huge market—according to some estimates, between $2 and $3 trillion a year in the United States. For more about how to sell to this market, check out *Cross-Cultural Selling For Dummies,* which I co-authored with cross-cultural selling expert Michael Soon Lee.

TRAIN YOUR MIND TO SPOT OPPORTUNITIES

Some people can naturally think of dozens of ways to market a product, but you don't need to be a born visionary. You can train your mind to look for business where it's not. Here are some suggestions that can open your mind to new sales and marketing opportunities:

- *Look for problems.* As explained in Week 15, every problem opens at least one and usually more business opportunities. By discovering the product or service that can solve a client's problem, you make a sale and have the opportunity to earn a client for life.

- *Talk to people.* Whether you are talking shop or just socializing, tune your ear to become more sensitive to the problems that people mention. If you hear a frustrated tone of voice, you can usually follow it to the source to discover a problem. Talking to people can also open you up to partnerships that may lead to other markets.

- *Read everything.* Reading articles, especially articles that seem to have nothing to do with what you're selling, can often make your mind more receptive to opportunities.
- *Travel.* Travel brings you in contact with people, places, products, services, and ideas that may not exist in the world in which you live. In addition, it changes your perspective, which often results in new ideas.

BUILD BUSINESS SYNERGIES

One of the best ways to come up with new ideas and tap into unserved and underserved markets is to team up with businesses and salespeople who offer complementary products and services. As a real estate agent, I have plenty of informal partnerships with title companies, mortgage brokers, attorneys, home inspectors, contractors, and others in my industry and related industries. Together, we can provide a complete menu of services to our clients.

As spokesperson for Blogging Systems (www.bloggingsystems .com), a turnkey solution for real estate agents who want a quick and easy way to establish a presence on the Internet, I am able to use my reputation and contacts to help Blogging Systems market its services while helping my colleagues discover easy ways to market themselves online.

I also reach outside my industry to build more creative business synergies. By becoming involved in Face to Face Live (a company that provides high-quality, affordable videoconferencing solutions), I have discovered remarkable new ways to streamline my own business operations and extend my market reach. At the same time, the folks at Face to Face Live are discovering new applications for their systems in the world of real estate.

Think of what you're selling and what you can add without having to do any more work. Make sure you're not getting yourself into a conflict-of-interest situation and that the partnership offers your clients a real value-add.

Ralph's Rule: Expose yourself to everything. The more exposure you have to everything life has to offer, the more resources your mind acquires to come up with creative new ideas.

WEEK 19

BRAINSTORM PROBLEM SOLVING WITH YOUR STAFF

S everal years ago, I started Summit Title, my own title company. Because every real estate transaction involves a title search, I thought this would be a natural extension of my brokerage work. I studied the market and hired a good staff and a great manager, who was a top salesperson in her own right.

We had a great opening month, and I thought I was a genius. Then the slide began. Our company wasn't yet well established. We had no customer base, and many of our new salespeople were inexperienced. We didn't have enough cash coming in to cover overhead, and pretty soon we had a serious problem on our hands.

I talked to my in-house lawyer, Peter Allen, who had helped me start Summit Title, and we went back and forth over whether we ought to close it down at once or try something else. I hated the idea of closing it. It was one of my babies, my pet projects, and I really believed that it would work. But I couldn't ignore the red ink, either, so we discussed how best to cut back without gutting the operation.

Rumors got around to the staff, and our manager came to me and said her staff wouldn't agree to take 20 percent pay cuts. I told her I didn't expect them to, but that some cutbacks were probably necessary. We just hadn't figured out what yet. A couple of hours later, she returned to my office. "Ralph," she said, "instead of laying off people, fire me. Don't pay me this big administrative salary. I'll become a salesperson."

I said something like, "You've got to be kidding. You're supposed to run the show." And she said, "Who's the best salesperson on the team? I am, right?" And I had to admit that she was right.

I went home and talked to Kathy, my wife, who actually owned the business at the time. She agreed with our manager. "Your job isn't to micromanage these operations, Ralph," she told me. "That's what you have a manager for—to manage."

So the solution to our problem at Summit Title was to let our manager quit and come back as a salesperson. She was happier doing deals again (and actually earning more money in commissions than she had earned in salary as a manager). We trimmed our costs substantially, and we were able to save the firm.

This story illustrates several points about problem solving. Everyone knows you have to "think outside the box." But how many of us actually do it? In this case, we had two guys with years of experience (me and my lawyer, Peter) basically coming up with the same old solutions—cut costs by firing people or shut down the operation. Both of these were very uncreative and unproductive solutions. It took our manager to come up with a much more creative solution—one that was good for the company and everyone involved.

In this chapter, I offer some tips on how to brainstorm with staff to develop creative, productive solutions.

ASK FOR HELP

As soon as you encounter a problem you cannot solve immediately, start talking about it. No single individual is as intelligent as a group. Talk to other team members and managers. If you work for a large company, talk to people in other departments. Remember, if the problem concerns everyone, then everyone should be part of the solution.

I know how salespeople hate to give up any control or show weakness. Doing whatever is necessary to solve a problem, however, gives you more control and enables you to overcome the weakness that the problem is causing. Assuming the staff you've assembled is as smart and talented as you think they are, don't neglect this amazing resource you have.

DON'T GET HUNG UP ON HIERARCHY

Along with asking for help, remember to think beyond the normal lines of authority. Department heads are not the only ones with good ideas. In fact, the people further down the line, the ones who are closer to the problem, often know best how to solve difficult issues.

FOSTER A PROBLEM-SOLVING ATMOSPHERE

In my office, I try to delegate as much as possible. I try to create systems to handle volumes of work, and then I delegate to others, as much as possible, the running of these systems. I often tell people not to involve me in minor details or everyday problem solving. For one thing, I need to stay upbeat and focused on my main job—selling—and I can't afford to get caught in a trap of negativity over minor problems. But, beyond this, I like to let other people get creative in their daily jobs. The solutions tend to be better, and the team happier, than if I'm trying to micromanage all the time.

THINK ENDS, NOT MEANS

Many of the arguments we have around the office really concern means, not ends. Everyone wants to succeed and make money. But it's surprising how often we disagree on how. To the extent that I can, I try to hear someone's argument in terms of the end result, not whether I happen to agree with his immediate focus. As long as he gets to where I want him to go, it really doesn't matter which path he follows.

There are all kinds of reasons that we get caught up in unproductive problem solving. Maybe it's ego, or fear of delegating, or a dozen other things. But if you involve others in your search for answers and get beyond those simplistic solutions that are generally ineffective or just plain wrong, you'll be surprised at the results.

Ralph's Rule: Just as you train to make presentations, you have to train yourself to think creatively to solve problems. Begin today. It's a skill well worth acquiring.

WEEK 20

FOCUS ON YOUR CLIENTS' SUCCESS

You strive to be successful. This is certainly under-standable and admirable, but it can bog you down. You can become so focused on the *bottom line* that you forget about your *top line*—your clients—and then both your bottom line and top line and everything in-between come crashing down.

I often see the negative effects of bottom-line thinking in sales de-partments. A manager sets a sales quota, and the sales staff becomes so focused on meeting the quota that they stop serving the clients. Even worse is when the client becomes aware that the salesperson needs to meet a quota by a certain date—this gives the client the upper hand at the negotiating table, forcing the salesperson to cave in to unrealistic demands just to make a quota.

You can use sales quotas as a way to measure your progress and inspire you to work more diligently to serve your clients, but they should never take your focus off of what is most important—your clients' success. In this chapter, I shift the focus from your success to the success of your clients.

YOUR SUCCESS IS MY SUCCESS

I write books. I mentor. I coach. I have earned a reputation as some-one who makes other people more successful. Nothing is more rewarding to me than to hear that a strategy or technique I passed along to someone improved his or her business.

I always introduce myself to everyone I meet for the first time, especially when I travel. I tell them my name, what I do, and what I sell, and then I ask about them. On one trip, I flew into Los Angeles and had booked a room at the Ritz Carlton, Laguna, Niguel, about an hour and fifteen minutes from the airport. On my way to the hotel, I struck up a conversation with the taxi driver. As usual, the driver asked me what I did for a living, and I explained that I sold real estate.

When he heard I was in sales, he wanted to know what he could do to increase sales. He wanted to sell more rides to the airport. I asked if I could see his business card. He replied that he didn't have one, so I said, "The first thing you need to do is have business cards printed up with your cell phone number on them, so people could call you directly instead of having to go through the dispatcher." I wrote down his cell phone number, so I could call him whenever I needed a ride during my eight-day stay.

The next day, I called the driver directly. When he arrived to pick me up, he handed me his new business card. I was pleasantly surprised to see that he had put my first suggestion into practice so quickly. He asked me if I had any other suggestions to boost his business.

I noticed that he had bucket seats in the front of his cab, so I said, "If I were you, I'd put a TV/DVD player between the seats and play movies. Your passengers could watch a movie on the drive from the airport to the hotel."

He wasn't too impressed with this suggestion. He replied, "But the ride is only an hour and fifteen minutes. They'd only be able to watch half the movie."

"Exactly," I said. "Then they'll have to call you for the ride back to the airport if they want to see the second half of the movie!"

Months later, I called the taxi driver to see how everything was working out for him. He was now running his own limousine service in Laguna.

SUCCESS BREEDS SUCCESS

The more people I help, the more people seek my help. If this book makes you more successful, you are likely to recommend it to other people you know who could benefit from it. When you want to learn even more about sales success, you will be more likely to order other books and training materials I have developed or hire me to coach you. The more successful I make you, the more successful I become.

This is true in any profession, but it is particularly relevant in sales. The more successful you can make your clients, the more they will rely on you to provide them with products and services and the more likely they are to refer you to others.

YOUR MISSION STATEMENT

As a salesperson, part of your mission statement should be, "Your success is my success." If you can help make your clients more successful, you benefit in at least three ways:

- Your clients will be more willing to purchase from you again.
- Your clients will have more money to purchase more products or services from you in the future.
- Your clients will send more referral business your way.

When you are on a mission to build your clients' success, this may mean that you don't make a particular sale. You may even send the client to one of your competitors, if your competitor is better equipped to meet the client's needs. Remember, you are building a reputation and relationships that will draw business to you throughout your career. Losing one sale is a small price to pay for establishing a positive relationship that will pay dividends for many years to come.

Ralph's Rule: As you discovered in Week 5, goal setting is an excellent motivational tool, but never let your goals take your focus off what is most important—your clients. Serve your clients well, and your goals will take care of themselves.

WEEK 21

WRITE NOTES TO YOUR CLIENTS

Most salespeople send thank-you notes and Christmas cards to their clients. It's a nice way to stay in touch, and it keeps your name in front of your clients. Unfortunately, most of these greetings are utterly routine—the same boring Christmas cards and the same impersonal thank-you notes that every salesperson sends. Most wind up in the garbage without a second thought.

Over the years, I've developed a unique mailing strategy that has become an important marketing tool for me. I want my mailings to send a message that I'm an informed, concerned salesperson—someone who really cares about my client's well-being. That may sound like a tall order, but here are six ways that you can elevate your mailing above the routine:

1. *Don't send cards on the same holidays everyone else does.* Everybody sends Christmas cards and birthday cards. I don't like to get lost in the pack. I send cards to my clients on less traditional holidays, like the Fourth of July instead of Christmas. I've even sent out cards on Groundhog Day. Few, if any, other salespeople remember these occasions, so I really stand out when I do. I credit my friend Stanley Mills, one of the top real estate agents in Tennessee, for teaching me this technique.

2. *Send a note even when you don't get the sale.* We all send thank-you notes when we close a deal. (At least I hope you're all doing that by now!) But I will often send a note even when the deal falls through. I just want clients to know that I'm still in the market and that I will be for many years to come. You never know when they'll need the services of a salesperson again. Often, the deal they've inked with somebody else falls through, and in those cases, I'm usually the first one they call simply because I've gone to so much trouble to stay in touch with them.

3. *Send a note when you've been quoted in the news media.* I take a lot of time to organize my press clippings. I like to send out copies by the thousands. Often I'll scribble a little note that says, "Thought you might be interested in this issue." Many of your competitors will send out simple thank-you notes, but hardly any of them will send a copy of a press clipping. It's another way to help you stand out from the pack.

4. *Send a note after you've met someone new.* We're constantly meeting new people, and I always carry around marketing material with me to give them. I hand out a couple thousand of my personal brochures a year to all sorts of people—restaurant servers, valet car parkers, people I meet at weddings and funerals. If, for some reason I can't give something to them right away, I'll ask for a business card from them and send something to their home or office. Remember, a salesperson succeeds in direct proportion to the number of people who know him. Even if your new acquaintance doesn't seem like an immediate prospect, they may turn into prospects later. Sooner or later everyone needs a car, a home, a computer, clothes, insurance, or whatever you sell.

5. *Send mail as a way to generate different kinds of income streams.* In my office, we've developed a multitude of products that have proven helpful to both my clients and other salespeople. For clients, these include reports on "How to Ready Your Home for Sale" or "How to Buy a House with No Down Payment." For salespeople, I generate training tapes and publications like "The 10 Biggest Mistakes I've Ever Made," outlining how I've turned errors into a winning strategies. Many of my mailings include information on how to buy these products. So the

mailing accomplishes two things. It keeps my name before the public while generating income.

6. *Send out lots of different kinds of mailings.* My mailings to clients include thank-you notes, birthday cards, press clippings, holiday greetings, follow-ups on previous contacts, and a whole lot more. You can turn almost anything into an occasion for a mailing. In my office, we mass mail an entire marketplace every month or so. It computes to hundreds of thousands of pieces of mail per year. But it's all worth it because by now I'm the best-known salesperson in my market. When people think of buying or selling a home, I'm the one they think of first.

And here's one more hint. With all the good contact-management software on the market today, generating mail for your clients can be as easy as typing a message and clicking a button. Don't pass up this outstanding way to stay in touch with your market.

Ralph's Rule: Just because most other salespeople use a certain technique doesn't mean you can't develop a unique version of your very own. Sometimes a small adjustment to the way everyone else is doing it can make a big difference. Try it!

LAUNCH YOUR WEEKLY HOUR OF POWER—100 CALLS IN 60 MINUTES

E very weekday, I spend one hour making 100 phone calls. I call it my *Hour of Power.* I select a group of people I want to contact. The group may consist of the people I work with on the *Macomb County Voice* (a community blog we created). It might be the top-selling real estate agents I know through Star Power. It might be talking with Power Team Leaders across the country, Macomb County Habitat for Humanity Board Members, community leaders, or coaching clients. It might be people I sold houses for or those I sold houses to. I tell everyone in the office that my Hour of Power is about to commence, and they know not to disturb me. Then, I shut myself in my office and start dialing.

If someone answers, I deliver my energetic greeting, ask them how they're doing, and perhaps mention one of the details I've recorded in my contact-management program; maybe it's their anniversary or one of their children's birthdays. If nobody answers, I move on to my next call. If I get the answering machine, I leave a message. I may even sing "Happy Birthday," wish the person a happy St. Patrick's Day, or say something goofy right off the top of my head that I think will make them smile.

(I learned the Happy Birthday Call from Stanley Mills of Crye-Leike Real Estate in Memphis, Tennessee. When I shadowed Stanley, he would print off a sheet of everyone's birthdays and anniversaries for the month. He would keep the list above his visor in his car, making the calls and never once mentioning real estate.)

HARVESTING PEARLS CALLED *REFERRALS*

The goal of the Hour of Power is to increase your referral business—gathering the pearls called *referrals*. It's about leveraging the power of the *Rule of 250*. According to this rule, each person knows at least 250 other people they can tell about you. No matter what you are selling, the Hour of Power is a proven method for increasing your return and referral business.

Far too many salespeople fail to leverage the power of satisfied customers. They spend a great deal of time and energy satisfying the customer, and then they toss away that huge investment by losing contact with the person. As a result, they spend time and energy in a constant pursuit of new customers.

Keep in mind that you already *earned* the respect of every customer you have satisfied. Your customers may not know how to thank you, so give them the best way possible to thank you: by sending referrals your way.

Unfortunately, customers and clients often forget even the best purchase experiences they've had. With the Hour of Power, you deliver a subtle reminder. You keep the experience alive in their minds. When that customer is talking with someone who is in the market for whatever you sell, he or she will recommend you without hesitation. You become synonymous with what you sell.

NO SELLING!

What you say during your Hour of Power phone calls isn't that important, but it should never be about selling—*no selling*. The

Hour of Power is about connecting on a personal level and keeping your name and face and what you sell fresh in the minds of all the people you know.

When you connect with people (or their answering machines), let them know that you've been thinking about them. If a holiday is near, wish them a happy holiday or ask whether they have any plans for the holiday. If they are married, ask how their wife or husband is doing. If their anniversary is approaching, wish the person a happy anniversary. The key is to remind the people you call that you still exist and that *you* are thinking about *them.*

Remember that your other marketing efforts are no replacement for the personal touch. You may be doing all the right high-tech marketing with web sites, blogs, drip e-mail campaigns, and print marketing, but all of that cannot possibly match the power of your own voice.

NO INTERRUPTIONS!

When you are doing your Hour of Power, you must not be interrupted. Make sure anyone who may be tempted to interrupt you knows not to. If you work in an office, tell the receptionist and everyone else within earshot that you will be incommunicado for one solid hour. If you sell from home, tell your partner (and any children you may have) that you are not to be disturbed.

If someone returns a call in response to a message you left on his or her answering machine during your Hour of Power, *the call counts as an interruption. Don't answer it.* Someone else in your office should answer the call and take a message. There must be *no interruptions.*

You can call the person back later, after the hour is up. Your goal is to make it through your list of 100 people, and you have only 60 minutes to do it.

KEEP A TALLY SHEET

As business starts to pick up—and it will, assuming you put your Hour of Power into practice—you will naturally start attending to other things and set your Hour of Power to the side. Some salespeople don't even make it to that point. They run out of steam after the first couple of days, long before they can reap the benefits of the Hour of Power.

For any technique to work, however, you need to do it and keep doing it. Create an Hour of Power tally sheet, and track the number of calls you make each day. Total the calls for a weekly and monthly count. This will help you stay on track.

Ralph's Rule: 100 phone calls in 60 minutes may sound overly ambitious, and perhaps it is a little beyond reach, but that's part of why it works. By compressing the time you allow yourself to complete the task, you force yourself into "the zone," and can be incredibly productive. When you begin, you may be making only 25 phone calls in 60 minutes, but keep at it. Soon, you will see that number rise and, along with it, your number of return and referral transactions will soar.

MASTER THE 10-10-20 TECHNIQUE

O ne of the not-so-secret secrets to sales success is to build on past success. This is what the Hour of Power, discussed in Week 22 is all about. It's also what the 10-10-20 technique is all about, but instead of calling past clients, you introduce yourself to 40 people who are closely associated with one of your clients.

I have used the 10-10-20 technique myself and have recommended it to many of my coaching clients. It works wonders for me, and my clients have reported similar results. It should work for you as well.

THE TECHNIQUE

Although the 10-10-20 technique boosts sales for just about anything marketable, I developed it for selling residential real estate. As such, the technique goes like this: When you list or sell a house, knock on the 10 doors to the left and right of the house you just sold and the 20 doors across the street and distribute your postcard with a handwritten note letting the neighbors know that you have listed or sold their neighbor's home.

That is it. That is all it takes to start generating new clients. It should take you less than an hour. Most of the neighbors are not going to want to talk with you at length. In less than an hour you have the potential of reaching 10,000 people.

Whoa! Where did that 10,000 number come from? According to my estimates, from attending weddings, anniversaries, graduations, and family reunions every person knows at least 250 other people. By contacting 40 people in the area, you indirectly contact nearly 10,000 more, and everyone in sales, particularly in real estate, knows that selling is all about meeting people and building relationships.

ANOTHER WAY TO NETWORK

The 10-10-20 technique is just another way to network, but this form of networking is much less formal than most and creates a grass-roots marketing campaign that spreads like a virus. As the neighbors begin to talk about that agent who had the courtesy to knock on their doors and let them know what was going on with that house that was for sale down the street, word will begin to spread far and wide, and prospective clients will begin calling.

CASE STUDY

I recently shared the 10-10-20 technique with a coaching client of mine Domenic Manchisi (www.domenicmanchisi. com). An excellent student, Domenic actually practices what I teach. He even decided to add a little of his own flair to the technique. After he helps clients find and purchase the home of their dreams, he takes a photograph of them in front of their new home and places the photo on the postcard that he hands out to the neighbors. This nice touch helps introduce the new family to the neighborhood.

(continued)

CASE STUDY *(Continued)*

Domenic reports that the response has been overwhelming. As soon has he sells one house, he has two more listing appointments waiting for him. According to Domenic:

> The people who are home when I go to the door are very impressed, as no other agent in my community does this. The sellers love it and see firsthand how hard I work for my clients.
>
> Recently in my hometown of Milton, Ontario, we had a home show—a three-day event held in the local sports arena showcasing local businesses. My office, Prudential Town Center Realty, had a booth, and my team had a majority of the floor time. We handed out my personal brochure along with a copy of our *Marketwatch* newsletter and spoke to everyone who walked by.
>
> At the time of the home show, I had been doing the 10-10-20 for about a month and I was surprised at the recognition I got just for that. Many people commented on me coming to their door. My marketing campaign to my farm of 10,000 has been going on for four months. Between that and knocking on doors, everyone seems to know my name. I am really starting to see how all this comes together. Not only am I enjoying the experience of getting out in the community and meeting my neighbors, but my profile in the business community is also growing.

Although you can hand out business cards, the postcards are something a little different and less business-oriented and they give you more flexibility to add a personal touch like Domenic did.

ADJUST THE TECHNIQUE

If you sell something other than houses or insurance, knocking on the neighbors' doors may not work as well for you as it does for real estate agents and insurance agents. However, you can adapt the technique to your industry.

Whenever you make a sale, try to obtain the customer's mailing address. Then, do some research to find the addresses of the person's neighbors—the 10 people who live on either side and the 20 who live across the street. You can then send these people memorable gifts, such as the following, depending on your industry:

- If you sell cars, consider sending prospective customers a tire gauge or a tin of chocolate chip cookies—who doesn't like chocolate chip cookies?

- A massage therapist might give regular clients a gift certificate to pass along to someone they know—a free half-hour massage, for example.

- If you're a caterer, prepare some extra food so there will be some leftovers—referrals will come in.

Ralph's Rule: The 10-10-20 technique is a very effective guerilla marketing maneuver. Although it does hearken back to the days of the door-to-door salesperson, in this case, you're not really selling anything, so people are less defensive. You're just getting to know your neighbors and letting them know what you can do for them.

WEEK 24

HONE YOUR NETWORKING SKILLS

I am firmly convinced that networking is the heart and soul of every sales career. If you can't network, you shouldn't be in sales. If you can't ask your family, friends, and total strangers for an order, choose another line of work.

Over the years, I've refined my approach to networking. I've kept some things, discarded others. By now, after some 30 years in sales, I've instilled the essence of my experience into my "Top 10 Tips," which are listed below. These are, in my opinion, 10 clear steps to better networking:

1. *There's no way around it—you have to network with everyone.* You have to network at your kid's school, when you go out to eat, and even when you stop at highway tollbooths. Give your business card to *everyone* you meet. Ask everyone for an order and/or referral.

2. *When you network, give something to everybody.* Your gift can be a business card or brochure, a flower, or even candy. Here's an example: Once upon a time, I parked my car with a valet. He showed me a brochure I had given him during a previous

visit. It really got me excited that he had saved my brochure and knew exactly where he kept it, so I looked in my truck and gave him a copy of an inspirational book called *The Platinum Rule* by Art Fettig, which I routinely give to hundreds of people a year. People remember you more often if you hand them something.

3. *Don't be afraid of being a little silly or unconventional.* When I go to a sports event, I've been know to throw a thousand business cards into the stands. Does even one of those cards ever come back to me as an order? I'll never know. But it sure feels great to know so many people have been exposed to my name.

4. *When you attend service club meetings like Rotary, don't always sit with the same five friends.* I know you feel more comfortable sitting with familiar faces. But unless you network more widely, you'll be limiting your opportunities to those same five people.

   Most service clubs have rules against giving your business cards except on specific occasions. They may fine you for openly asking for business because these clubs are supposed to be more social. But I've found that the more fines I paid, the more business I got. I just hand out my cards all the time at service clubs and cheerfully pay my fines. It's a great form of cheap advertising.

5. *Referrals work from the top down, not the bottom up.* A boss may pass along the name of a salesman to an employee, but it usually doesn't happen the other way around. So when you network, try to network at the highest level possible. If you're networking car dealers, for example, network the dealership owner before the guy in the body shop. The owner will be in a better position to pass your name along to others.

6. *Join or start your own tip or lead club.* Tip or lead clubs meet every week, and their members try to generate leads for each other. I've joined some lead clubs and started some. You'll get lots of ideas from them and you can network with the other members.

7. *Churches can be great places to network.* You've got an entire organization of people with like-minded beliefs. Try to put your ad in their weekly bulletin or newsletter. In fact, offer to pay for producing and mailing it in exchange for free ad space. It's worth every penny.

8. *You've got to be seen at all the major events.* At my level, I go to so many events—fund-raisers, community holiday parties, charitable events—it's hard to know which ones bring in new business. But I am convinced that every time I attend one of these events, especially if some radio personality interviews me, it adds to the bottom line in some way.

9. *Have a house account with restaurants where you can sign for meals and get billed monthly.* That way, maybe 10 different people at the restaurant see your name on the bill—the waiter, the cashier, the house accountant, secretaries, managers, everyone. And when you pay your bill, include your card or brochure.

10. *Get other people to network for you.* When I buy clothes, I tell the salespeople that the more successful I am, the more other people will ask me where I buy clothes, so it's in their best interest to network on my behalf. There's a shoeshine man in Detroit who automatically gives out my brochure every time someone getting a shoeshine mentions buying or selling a home.

Ralph's Rule: All these tips blend common sense with a little showmanship, but, believe me, they work. I have thousands of transactions to my credit that prove my point. I firmly believe that if you follow these tips, someday you'll be a top networker and salesperson yourself. Try it!

MARKET YOUR HOME-BASED BUSINESS

S tella Borst and Pam Lusczakoski are two women from suburban Detroit who can teach us all about marketing. They ran a business called Artistic Accents by Pastel from the basement of Stella's home. Their company sold stencils—a more sophisticated version of the old paint-by-number kits we had all used as kids. They sold these kits to homeowners, hobby shops, and interior decorators—anyone with an interest in brightening up a home or office.

Now, just because a business is home-based doesn't mean you can neglect marketing. In fact, you probably need to do more of it than ever. A home-based business doesn't have any storefront appeal; no one can window-shop because you don't have any store window for them to walk by. So you've got to get the word out in other ways.

Now, Stella and Pam were as good at this as anybody. They were entirely self-taught, too. "I don't have a degree in marketing," Stella once said. "We sit down here and say, 'Who can we pester now?' "

I'll describe a few of their marketing efforts here. I urge you to adopt some or all of these if you operate your own home-based business.

BARGAIN FOR AN ADVANTAGE

Stella and Pam were walking through a shopping mall when they saw a long blank wall. They quickly decided it would make an ideal display for their stencils. So they struck a bargain with the mall manager. In exchange for decorating the wall with stencils of flowers and trees and birdhouses and picket fences, the mall gave them a small kiosk from which to promote their stencil kits and catalogs. Their decorating efforts at the mall attracted a lot of attention and even made the local newspaper.

In a similar example, the women bargained with a national paint company. They agreed to include the company's brand of paint in the stencil kits in exchange for free promotion by the paint company.

I call these methods *zero-based marketing*. We use it all the time at my real estate firm. It's a way of getting other people who benefit from your efforts to help pay your marketing costs. For example, mortgage lenders tend to get a lot of referrals from me, so I've asked them to help pay the cost of producing my home advertising flyers. This brings down the cost of producing and mailing these flyers.

NICHE MARKETING

A lot of home-based firms make the mistake of plugging all their marketing dollars into one big ad in a large general-interest publication. That's a mistake. The ads usually don't work and you've blown your marketing budget.

Stella and Pam would spend carefully on ads in a variety of small publications devoted to home decorating. One was the *1001 Country Decorating Ideas,* a start-up publication that went to exactly the kinds of customers the women wanted to reach. And the two women weren't afraid to ask for extras. In exchange for a $300 ad, the magazine agreed to include a mention of them in an article.

SEEK FEEDBACK CONSTANTLY

Every time a customer ordered a catalog or a kit, Stella and Pam asked where the customer heard of Artistic Accents. They invested more marketing resources in whatever they found drew more customers.

This is a technique that I've used for years. I've tried all kinds of marketing—direct mail, billboards, TV, newspaper ads, the Internet, and much, much more. You've got to give a new marketing technique a few months to work and then evaluate it. If it's making you money or breaking even, continue it for another few months. If it's losing money, drop it. When you find something that works, stick with it for as long as it helps you.

BE CONSISTENT

Deciding they'd sell more kits if customers thought their stencils were easy to use, Stella and Pam emphasized that even beginners could be stenciling in 20 minutes. Every single piece of marketing underscored this ease of use.

Consistency is key. Most experts say you shouldn't begin a marketing campaign unless you're confident that you'll feel comfortable with the message 5 or even 10 years from now.

SET ASIDE TIME EVERY WEEK FOR MARKETING

Stella estimated that they would spend one day a week strictly on thinking up new marketing efforts and implementing them. Less savvy entrepreneurs market only during slack times. By making it a regular scheduled activity, Stella and Pam increased the odds they'd have fewer and briefer sales slumps.

These two women working in the basement of Stella's home could teach most entrepreneurs a lot about marketing. If you run a home-based business, I strongly urge you to adopt and adapt some of their methods to your own company. Good luck!

Ralph's Rule: Thinking of ways to attract new customers is a 24/7 activity for a home-business owner. You can never do enough marketing.

WEEK 26

MASTER A NEW TECHNOLOGY

Probably half the computer software purchased never gets used. It either sits in its shrink-wrapped box on a shelf at home, or maybe it gets loaded into a computer but never called up. Perhaps the buyer uses only a tiny piece of the software program, but never taps its full potential. What a waste.

It's sad because technology, if used properly, can boost your business to new heights of profit and productivity. Certainly this is what I have discovered at my own company here in Detroit. I never would have been able to reach the pinnacle of success without technology.

Over the years, I've developed some strategies for getting the most out of technology. In this chapter, I'll outline a few of them. Follow them and you'll do more than get the most from your computer, software, wireless devices, videoconferencing systems, and other technologies. You'll also find yourself steadily rising in the ranks of your profession:

1. *The first model introduced may stink, but improved versions follow quickly.* This works across a variety of technologies. Consider videoconferencing systems. Videoconferencing technology has been around for nearly half a century, but developers encountered a host of bottlenecks that prevented it from

becoming a practical technology. The video was fuzzy and choppy, phone lines did not have the bandwidth to carry massive amounts of audio and video data, and the systems were bulky, clunky, expensive, and highly unreliable. Now, even small businesses can afford to purchase high-quality, reliable, and user-friendly video conferencing systems, such as those offered by Face to Face Live (www.f2fl.com). I can now run my business in Washington Township, Michigan, and speak face to face with my operations manager who happens to live in Laguna Beach, California, just by placing a call.

Had I given up on videoconferencing because the first systems were expensive and hard to use, I would never have enjoyed the many improvements that have come along since.

2. *Any technology has more than one use, so learn them all.* Take, for example, all the new features that phone companies offer. Many people use only a couple available features, such as voice mail, and never explore some of the more high-end features, such as call forwarding. They may not even use voice mail to its full potential. Here are some ways to make the most of your phone system(s) and other communication tools:

- Use voicemail as a proactive tool. Many top salespeople change their greetings every morning. This lets callers know that you are in the office and interested in their calls.

- Use call forwarding to have phone calls automatically forwarded to your cell phone when you are on sales calls.

- Consider using a service that forwards voice calls to you via e-mail, so you can have on-demand access to your voice mail through your e-mail program.

- Purchase a wireless device, such as a Blackberry or iPhone, to handle all of your communication needs, including voice calls and e-mail.

- Learn to send and receive text messages on your cell phone, so you can more effectively communicate with clients who prefer this method of keeping in touch.

- Call your phone company about the availability of an interactive toll-free system. Callers can browse through a menu or order products, such as my customer guides to buying a home. On the system I use at my office, callers can ask for information about mortgage loans, and the employee in charge of my mortgage operation will be paged immediately. He can return the call within moments. I can also use the system to weigh the effectiveness of my advertising because callers key in a code that they've seen in a given ad.

3. *Sometimes the best technology purchase is more of the same thing.* I have several computers working for me at once. One is connected to the Internet at all times, sending and receiving e-mail, searching for and downloading the latest news and reports, and making sure my web sites and blogs are up to date. Another keeps track of my calendar and contacts, so I never miss an important meeting or event. The other is set up for doing word processing. I can quickly pivot on my office chair from one computer to the other without missing a beat. As long as you learn how to use the technology to perform practical tasks rather than getting caught up in the technology itself, the more technology you have, the more efficient you become. Change is accelerating, and I want to stay on top of it.

4. *Older technologies sometimes are best.* Consider the telephone. Far too many people have become overly reliant on other communications technologies, including e-mail and text messaging. Children and adolescents are growing up with these new technologies and honing their text-based communications skills, which is excellent, but more and more of them are experiencing the limitations of this mode of communication. They have to learn that text messaging is more literal—it often fails to convey the context and the feeling behind the message—which often leads to misunderstandings.

I still find myself picking up the phone and calling people rather than relying solely on e-mail, particularly when I need to resolve a sensitive issue. To me, this old communications technology is light years beyond the newer technologies, simply because it allows people to remain human and communicate on a more personal level. Of course, I am relying more and more on my videoconferencing system because it enables me to communicate not only verbally but also through my gestures and facial expressions.

I also still rely on voice recorders to take notes and compose memos, but now, instead of using my old Dictaphone, I use a digital recorder, which also comes with speech-recognition software that can help translate my spoken words into text.

5. *The best technology is one you use.* Don't be like the people who can't figure out how to record TV shows, never upgrade their software, or leave their computer back at the office. If you don't use it, why buy it in the first place? If you put all your technology to the very best use, you'll find your sales and income soaring.

Ralph's Rule: Learn what your current technology has to offer and use it. Check out the newer technologies regularly. But make sure you will gain from it before buying it. Technology that isn't used to your benefit is useless.

WEEK 27

EXPLORE MARKETING OPPORTUNITIES ON THE INTERNET

I f you are not marketing on the Internet, you are missing out on a huge slice of the retail pie. According to the 2006 U.S. Census Bureau E-Stats report, eCommerce in the retail sector accounted for over $100 billion in annual sales. And this does not account for the millions of customers who shop online but purchase offline. More and more people do their preliminary research on the Web before they ever get serious about buying anything, especially big-ticket items, including homes, cars, boats, computers, entertainment centers, and just about everything else you can imagine.

In addition, people are constantly searching for tips and tricks on how to get the most out of what they purchased, how to repair or maintain equipment, where to go for a great vacation, where to live, and much, much more. The people who provide the information that is in high demand often have an inside track to a particular market.

By establishing a presence on the Internet and building a reputation as the go-to guy or gal for information related to your industry and the products and services you sell, you position yourself to become the salesperson of choice when a prospect is in the market for what you sell. In the following sections, I discuss various ways to increase your presence on the Internet.

BUILD YOUR OWN WEB SITE

You should have at least one web site you call home. This web site should provide an online version of your marketing packet, including a photo of you (on the front page), your contact information, information about you and what you do and what you sell, information about your company, and perhaps a link to research or purchase the products and services you sell. I have several web sites, including AboutRalph.com, where interested parties can meet me and find out what I have to offer; RalphRoberts.com, where home buyers or sellers can find out about Ralph Roberts Realty; and FlippingFrenzy.com, which is really a blog designed to educate consumers and professionals about the problems associated with real estate and mortgage fraud. (For more about blogs, see Week 37.)

Register Your Own Domain

A domain is a specific place on the Internet, for example, foreclosureselfdefense.com. While some companies, including Yahoo! allow you to set up a free personal web site, they usually require that you include their domain as part of your domain name—for example, yourname.yahoo.com. By registering your own domain, you have a unique address of your very own where your clients can always find you.

Choose a domain name that people can remember easily and preferably one that reflects your name, such as RalphRoberts.com. (You can have several domain names that all point to the same web site, so you may want to register any domain names that are similar to your name.)

You can easily check domain name availability (for free) and register domain names online (for about $10 per domain name per year, assuming the domain name is not already registered). Visit online Web hosting services such as GoDaddy.com, Bluehost.com, and Register.com for more information about domain names and hosting services.

Subscribe to a Reliable Web Hosting Service

A Web hosting service stores your web site on a server that provides visitors with access to your site. Hosting costs vary, but most services charge less than $100 for a full year of service that includes several e-mail accounts, web site management tools, and a host of other tools to build and manage your web sites and blogs. You can manage several domains through a single account, so the cost of adding an additional domain later is only $10 a year (or whatever the service charges for domain registration). You do not need to set up a separate account for each domain.

Tip: Most Web hosting services partner with professional web site design companies and can recommend a professional designer. If you go with a pro, you can expect to pay about $5,000 for the initial web site design and setup.

Plan Carefully

You can probably slap together a decent looking web site in an hour or two, but you can avoid a great deal of frustration and rework by setting it up properly the first time. I strongly recommend that you use a content management system (CMS), such as WebYep (www.obdev.at/products/webyep). A typical CMS provides a collection of tools that enable you to create and edit Web pages online (inside your browser window) that you can later simply pull up in your browser and edit just as if you were editing a document in a word processor or desktop publishing program.

If you do not create your web site using a CMS, trying to add a CMS later can be a nightmare. The more planning you do up front, the less fiddling you will need to do later, and the easier it will be to modify the web site, if necessary.

BUILD COMMUNITIES THROUGH BLOGGING

Blogs (short for Web logs) give you the opportunity to quickly and easily post messages to the Web. A blog usually has one or more templates you can choose from (or customize) that control the appearance and function of everything on your blog. You simply choose the desired template.

Posting content to your blog is simply a matter of typing the information into a form. You type a title for your post and then the desired contents and then click a button (usually the Publish button). The article is then posted to your blog where visitors can read and comment on it. You'll learn more about blogs in Week 37. For now, realize that blogs are powerful but relatively simple tools for building communities, gaining visibility with search engines (such as Google), and marketing yourself as an expert in your industry.

DRIVE TRAFFIC TO YOUR WEB SITES AND BLOGS

Soon after you have a web site to market yourself and your business, you need to start promoting it. Once people begin to visit your site and talk about it, word-of-mouth advertising will drive traffic to your site, but people have to know about your site first.

Set a goal of getting a million people to your web site. While that may seem unrealistic, I prefer that you set your goal a little on the high side. Then, create a list of the various ways you can get that many people to visit your site, such as:

- *Post valuable content.* Content is king. People will not return to your site if it does not offer something fresh and valuable.

- *Add a Google sitemap.* A Google sitemap helps Google and other search engines catalog the content on your site. For details, visit www.google.com/webmasters/sitemaps.

- *Add Google Analytics.* Google Analytics is a nifty tool that enables you to track traffic coming into and moving through your site. You can see where visitors are coming from, which pages they're pulling up most frequently, the percentage of new and returning visitors, and much more. This helps you find out which content is popular and which is not, so you can provide people more of what they're looking for. For additional details, visit www.google.com/analytics.

- *Register with niche directories.* Page rankings are often determined by the number of "important" web sites in your web site's category that link to your site. By registering your site with industry-related directories, you can boost your page rank, so that when people use Google and other search engines to search for industry-related terms, your page is more likely to pop up higher on the list. For a great list of niche directories, visit Incoming Links at www.incominglinks.com.

- *Post messages in industry-related discussion forums or blogs.* By contributing to community discussions, you automatically increase your credibility. If the forum (or blog) allows members to include their web site or blog address in posts, this gives you another way of linking to your site from another site and increasing your search engine page rank.

- *Write articles and reviews for other web sites.* Offer to write articles and reviews for industry-related online publications. Most online publishers allow you to add a brief bio at the end of the article complete with a link back to your site.

ADD A SIGNATURE FILE TO YOUR E-MAIL MESSAGES

Every e-mail program enables you to have a *signature* automatically added to the end of every outgoing e-mail message. Use your e-mail program's signature option (in Outlook Express, choose Tools, Options, Signatures) to add a signature file including your name, contact information, and links to your web sites and blogs. If you e-mail me with a request at RalphRoberts@RalphRoberts.com, I will send you an e-mail that includes the signature file I use.

In addition to promoting your web sites and blogs, your signature file provides the recipient with instant contact information, including your phone number. While I am on the road, I often check e-mail messages with my BlackBerry. When I receive a message that contains a signature file, I can see the person's phone number and quickly call them without having to search for their phone number or call back to the office to get the phone number if I do not have it with me. By adding a signature file to outgoing e-mail messages, you make it easy for the recipient to get back in touch with you.

Ralph's Rule: Don't whine about the fact that the Internet is destroying your traditional way of doing business. That won't change the fact. Embrace the change and figure out how to put the Internet to work for you.

WEEK 28

REWARD YOURSELF

Everybody works for something. We exchange our time and expertise for money and other benefits, so we can take care of ourselves and our families and acquire some additional perks that make life worth living. Unless you reward yourself for your hard work every once in a while, you begin to feel as though you are working for nothing, and this can soon become very discouraging.

During this week of sales training, I encourage you to take a break to reward yourself for your efforts and dangle a few additional carrots in front of yourself to remain motivated for the remaining 24 weeks of the year.

CREATE A REWARD COLLAGE

My wife, Kathleen, and I are big on creating reward collages. Each of us envisions what we want—a new outfit, a new car, a vacation, whatever—and then we cut out pictures from magazines that remind us of our rewards and paste them onto a poster board. We then hang our boards in a prominent location of the house to remind ourselves of what we are working for. I encourage you to do the same.

At Ralph Roberts Realty, I once passed out 6-foot sheets of paper and rallied everyone in the office to create a massive collage of everything they envisioned that would make them happier—a new car, a new home, more time with family, a vacation, a garden... whatever they dreamed of. When I realized that I was one of only a few team members who was actually creating a collage, I offered everyone who completed their collage a $1,000 bonus.

Wayne Turner takes a different approach. He goes around to every person on his team and asks them, "If you had a day to just relax on your back porch and read magazines, which two magazines would you read?" He then heads to the store and buys everyone their favorite magazines, a medium-sized corkboard and a box of thumbtacks. After giving the team a couple of days to thumb through the magazines, they all gather with their scissors, magazines, and corkboards to create a collage of all the things they want in their lives—everything that brings them peace and happiness, whether it's a pool in the backyard, a new car or diamond ring, or time with family. It can even be a motivational phrase... anything that can keep you focused and on track. Everyone hangs their reward collages near their desks where they can glance at them every day for motivation.

Note: As I began my latest collage, my second in command, Lois, pointed out that what I find most rewarding is the success of those around me. Now, my collages are populated with photos and other reminders of the people around me.

REWARD YOURSELF BEFORE A SALE

Most salespeople reward themselves *after* they close a deal or meet their sales goals for a certain period. I do that, too, but to mix it up, I occasionally reward myself *before* I have achieved by goal.

Let me explain. I work hard to give my family a good life. I pay my mortgage, just like you, but I always try to create some other reason why I have to keep working. Call it creative tension or whatever you like. Put simply, I like to see the rewards, and I know I work better and harder if I can see the rewards up front.

Sometimes, I'll clip out a picture of what I want and hang it above my desk to motivate me. Other times, though, I'll just buy myself some new suits or a barbecue grill or a hot tub for my yard—before I've got anything special to celebrate. Then I go out and make something happen in my business to pay for it.

My friend Stanley Mills, one of the top real estate salespeople in Tennessee, and Allan Domb, the condominium king of Philadelphia, both follow this practice. For sure, it's not necessarily the clothes or the car or the vacation in themselves that pump me up—it's the excitement they give me. Through a constant flow of gifts to myself and others, I see the tangible fruits of all my hard work, and that serves to make me work even harder.

FINE-TUNE YOUR REWARD SYSTEM

By now, I have developed my reward system to a fine degree. For example, I love to use money interest-free. The last time I bought a barbecue grill I filled out the store's credit application and got the grill for no money down and no interest for 90 days. Then I paid off the loan in full on the 75th day, because if you go over the 90 days the store will charge interest back to day one.

When I go Christmas shopping in Chicago each year, I often use interest-free credit in this same way. In fact, my goal during the two days we spend shopping in Chicago is to get one new credit card per day. Often the store will give you an extra 10 percent off the price of the item just for applying for the card. So I buy something I want and get a nice discount and do not have to pay anything for close to 90 days. I simply use the store's money interest-free. I just love that.

If you think that I must accumulate a lot of credit cards this way, you're correct. I now have many cards—almost all locked away in a vault for safekeeping. And I don't pay an annual fee on any of them. If a card issuer wants to charge me a fee, I cancel the card or just ask the issuer to waive the fee, which they often do.

There are other advantages of my reward system. Once I apply for a card, I get more catalogs delivered at home. I enjoy shopping by catalog, too.

Now, as I said, you have to be careful if you're not familiar with shopping this way. Too many people get in trouble with consumer debt. If you're not careful, it could lead to bankruptcy. As my beautiful but more conservative wife, Kathy, puts it: "If we both spend money excessively, we'd be in trouble."

But, with that caution, I have to emphasize that top salespeople like me use this method of rewarding ourselves as a key motivational tool. Most of us are in sales because we like to be able to buy nice things for ourselves and our families. Don't go crazy and don't buy in advance if you're not comfortable with that. But you need to establish a reward system for yourself. On those down days when nothing seems to be working, thinking ahead to the rewards you've promised yourself will motivate you to get back in there and sell.

Ralph's Rule: Envision the lifestyle you want and then prioritize your list of wants so you can focus your energies on a select few. Once you know what you want, work back from rewards to setting sales goals that would secure them.

WEEK 29

FIND A BETTER PLACE TO MEET YOUR CLIENTS

For many salespeople, the question of where a sales call takes place is a given. You sell clothing in a mall boutique and that's where you meet your customers. Or you sell boats at a marina and you meet buyers in the showroom or on the lot. Or you sell mortgages in a loan office and you talk to customers at your desk.

This is all well and good. But if, like me, you have some choice of where you meet customers, you ought to give some serious thought to getting this right. This seemingly innocent choice actually could make or break the success of your sales call.

CHOOSE A PLACE WITH THE RIGHT AMBIENCE

Let's start with a given. You always want to discover how your customer *feels* about a transaction, not what he or she *thinks* about it. Buying decisions are primarily emotional, gut reactions, and you want to learn what hopes, fears, expectations, and desires your customer harbors for whatever you're selling.

After many years of close observation, I firmly believe that some places are more conducive than others to bringing out a customer's true feelings. For example, when I'm meeting clients in their home, I always try to get them to the kitchen table as quickly as possible. People invite acquaintances or businesspeople to the living room or den, but they invite friends to the kitchen. That's where they're most likely to unwind. That's where they'll reveal their true feelings to me.

Sometimes I have to use a little fancy footwork to get to the kitchen. If I'm trying to get the listing to sell this home, and the customer invites me to sit in the living room, I may ask for a glass of water or simply say I want to see their kitchen. I use my gut instincts with each client to judge how easily and how quickly I can accomplish this initial aim of getting to the kitchen table. It doesn't always succeed, but it always makes my work easier when that's where we have our conversation.

SET THE STAGE

I think a lot about how to set the stage for my sales call, too. If I'm calling a husband and wife at their home, which I often do, I like to place my customers at the corner of the kitchen table, close together, with me at the opposite corner. This way I can see both of them at the same time. I can judge from their eyes and their body language how I'm doing.

You can adapt this principle to almost any setting. If you're meeting customers in a restaurant, try to get them to sit facing you, not facing the rest of the room. A busy restaurant offers so many distractions that your customers' attention may wander. You want them focused on you alone so you can draw them out about the transaction.

Even if you sell clothes in a mall, you can exercise some choice of setting. You could, for example, approach customers while they're at the clothes rack or stand back in a more reserved posture at the counter. To me, it seems clear that more sales are made at the rack than at the counter because at the rack you can get truer reactions, as well as demonstrate your expertise about the various lines of clothing. A sales representative who waits at the counter for customers to bring their selections is really just an order taker, not a salesperson in the true sense of the word.

NAVIGATE AN OFFICE MEETING

Suppose you make sales calls on companies. Maybe you'll be directed to the purchasing manager's office, or even to the desk of a subordinate. When possible, suggest that the meeting be held in the executive's private office. Maybe that's obvious, but let's examine why. Even a corporate conference room is not as good as a private office. Conference rooms are remote from the place where the purchasing executive feels comfortable. It's where group decisions are made, often in the negative because most committee decisions are negative.

Instead, you want to get inside that comfort zone, not in a threatening way, but just so the buyer will let his or her hair down a little and share with you some genuine reactions. At the very least, you may learn why you're not getting the deal at this time. Outside the comfort zone, your customer may have told you that the company just doesn't need your product right now, but in his office he may let you know he was disappointed with the service last time around. Such honest reactions are crucial to successful selling in the future.

By the way, when you call on a company, try to find out as much as you can about it and its structure. Get the names not only of the purchasing agent and the agent's boss, but also the names of the secretaries and the receptionist. Take my office, for example. Often another salesperson who's trying to sell me something will call and ask for Ralph, as though he knows me. My receptionist will say I'm not in the office, so the caller will ask, "Is Lois there?" referring to my second in command. Since the caller knows Lois's name, our receptionist will put the call through to her. Maybe we won't want to buy anything that day, but at least the caller knew enough to get a step closer to the decision maker in the office.

In the same way, the more you know about how a company works, the better the odds you'll be able to complete your sales call successfully.

Ralph's Rule: Sales success is a matter of details. I can think of no situation where you couldn't improve the odds in your favor by a little artful stage setting. Give the setting some thought, and I bet you will see results.

IMPROVE THE WAY YOU ASK AND ANSWER QUESTIONS

O ne of the themes of this book is that you must treat your clients with respect. Don't lie to them; don't try to manipulate them. Give them your very best advice and work for a long-term relationship, not for a short-term sale. This is the best advice I can give you.

At the same time, I don't want you to carelessly talk yourself out of a sale through verbal mistakes. There are good ways and bad ways to negotiate a deal. If a transaction is not in the clients' best interest, don't try to force it on them. But when a deal is exactly what they want and need, you still need to be careful not to upset the chemistry that has gotten your clients to the brink of saying yes.

I always practice a form of sales talk that emphasizes listening on my part and asking lots of questions. I never ask questions that a client can answer with a simple yes or no. One-word answers kill the conversation and they don't tell me anything. As a salesperson,

I've got to uncover my client's emotional reactions to the pending sale. My first rule of sales talk is discussed next.

ASK QUESTIONS THAT REQUIRE SOME EXPLANATION FROM YOUR CLIENT

For example, I never ask home sellers what price they want to list their house for.

That would get a reply like "$160,000." Instead, I'll ask what factors go into the clients' thinking about the price. They may tell me their friends down the street sold their house for that much. And now I understand more about their expectations and what I have to do to bring them around to a realistic price.

In the same way, I avoid giving simple, direct answers to many questions that clients ask me. And for the same reasons. I don't want to kill the conversation; rather, I'm looking for ways to draw out my clients so I can understand their feelings. For example, if the clients ask me what I think of a price of $175,000, instead of saying it's too high or too low for their house, I may say something like, "Tell me why that price appeals to you." The goal is to get the client talking about the concerns that lie behind their questions. Once you know those concerns, you're in a much better position to counsel your client.

TRY TO ANSWER A QUESTION WITH A QUESTION OF YOUR OWN

You've also got to be careful not to "unsell" your product. If the clients ask me how big a home lot is, I do not answer directly by saying "150 by 80." That may scare them off if they think that lot size is too big or too small. So I'll ask, "How big do you want it?" And they may say something like, "Not too big because I don't want to have to mow the lawn." And then I can say, "That's great because this lot is average for its neighborhood and not too big."

In the same way, if a caller asks how many bedrooms does this home have, the answer isn't three or four. The correct answer is, "How many bedrooms do you want?" If they say three, I can say, "Great, this home has three bedrooms and a den."

Even if your product isn't directly what the client wants, you can still answer questions by pointing out the advantages of what you're selling. Don't push so far that you annoy the client, but you need to guard against losing a deal that's good for your client by giving a careless answer.

BREAK DOWN BAD NEWS INTO TERMS THAT ARE EASIER TO ACCEPT

For example, suppose the clients tell me that a home price is $10,000 more than they think they can afford. Instead of saying the deal's over, I'll ask them what they think that $10,000 means in terms of a monthly payment. Maybe they have some exaggerated idea of what their monthly obligation would be. And I'll say, "What if I can show you that extra $10,000 means only $2 a day more in your payments? Or $60 a month?" Or something like that. I'll keep working with them to break down the scary-sounding number to something they can more easily handle.

Sometimes their fears or emotional reactions are based on erroneous thinking. And sometimes these fears can put them out of a sale that really could be good for them. It's our job as salespeople to make sure this doesn't happen. I don't want you to force any deals that are bad for your clients; but also I don't want you to let a good transaction get away simply because you ask or answer a question in a careless way.

Ralph's Rule: Talking to a client is an art form. It involves getting the client to reveal what he or she really feels about your product or service. If you can guide the conversation to that point, you'll find both you and your clients are happier.

WEEK 31

PERFECT YOUR TELE-SALES SKILLS

S everal years ago, my wife, Kathleen, was getting ready to celebrate a special birthday. I wanted to buy her the car of her dreams—a red Corvette. Since I didn't have time to go from showroom to showroom, I started making calls from my office each day. Unfortunately, every Corvette salesman I talked to refused to quote me a price over the phone. It was maddening. One would say, "We can't give you that over the phone, you'll have to come in," and I would say, "You know what? That's what the last salesperson who's not going to sell me a car today told me." Finally, I found a salesperson who said he had the car I want. He quoted me a price and said he'd hold it for me. "Great," I told him, "I'll be there in two hours." And in two hours when I arrived this guy told me that another customer had put down a deposit on the car and it was no longer available. I was steamed!

So far, this little story has been about how not to do telephone sales. Rude, evasive, unhelpful telephone calls benefit no one—not the salesperson and certainly not the customer. Yet telephone sales are a necessary part of almost any sales career today. You may believe, as I do, that face-to-face selling at a customer's kitchen table is better than selling by phone; face-to-face selling gives us a better feel for a customer's emotional reactions than telephone sales do.

But let's deal with reality. In this day of national and international accounts and high-volume business, selling by phone is a must.

As my story of Corvette shopping proves, however, there are right ways and wrong ways to do it. All those initial salespeople just turned me off to the idea of working with them. Think of how much money those salespeople lost by not being helpful over the phone.

Basically, the right way to do telephone sales remains the same as in face-to-face selling. You treat your customers with respect. You don't lie to them. You don't make promises you can't deliver, like that auto salesman I just told you about.

But let me finish my story. I returned to my office, and over the next couple of weeks I continued to search by phone for the right car. And finally I found a salesman by the name of Lew Tuller in a dealership in Dearborn, Michigan. I'm convinced that Lew is the best Corvette salesperson who ever lived. I told Lew what had occurred, and he made everything happen—quoted me the price, found the car, faxed me the credit application, everything. I couldn't have been happier.

What made the difference? Lew treated my telephone contact as a potential sale to be made right there on the phone—not as a tactic to get me into the showroom. He treated me as an intelligent buyer. As a result, he earned himself a fan for life.

Here, then, are my rules for successful telephone sales.

MAKE A LOT OF CALLS

Years ago I met a real estate agent named Allan Domb, the condominium king of Philadelphia, who makes 100 phone calls a day. I didn't think it was possible to make that many. So I went to Philly for a day to shadow Allan—just to watch him work. Through speed dialing and multiple phones and two secretaries to help him, Allan does indeed make his 100 calls a day. I was so impressed that I made that my own goal. I now have two telephones on my desk. If I'm on hold waiting for one call to go through, I'll often pick up the other and make a second call. Sometimes I have to juggle the receivers a bit, but it usually works out fine. You learned about my Hour of Power during Week 22.

From this experience I've uncovered a simple yet dynamic truth: The more calls you make, the more money you'll earn. It's a numbers game. The more contacts you make, the better chances you have of uncovering that customer who was just waiting for your call. Don't be afraid to keep calling back at regular intervals, either. Jim Good, one of America's best trainers of telemarketers, tells how a bottled water salesman visits his office every month or so. Jim has always turned him down. But eventually, Jim says, he's probably going to feel like buying bottled water just when that salesperson stops by. Telephone sales are the same thing. Keep calling and eventually someone will be in a mood to buy.

I tell my sales staff to make 25 calls a day in addition to all their other work. I can't set that as a goal for them unless I'm willing to go beyond that to set an example. And that's what I try to do with my 100 calls a day. I don't always reach that goal, but I always make dozens of calls.

That's my first rule: Make a lot of calls. The more you make, the richer you'll be.

NO SCRIPTS

Back in the 1970s, when I was starting out in sales, I read a lot of books on sales techniques that were popular then. Most of these books recommended specific things to say to customers in any situation. These were scripts to follow. And I'd call a customer and deliver one of these scripted lines and the customer would say, "Those are the exact same words that the other salesman said to me yesterday." People can tell when you're not sincere. They can tell when you're just delivering a line.

So stay away from canned remarks. Write your own, original material. Inject your calls with your own personality, whether over the phone or in person, and you will receive a much warmer welcome.

THE "MIRRORING" TECHNIQUE

When you're on the phone, you don't have your customer's body language to read, so you have to find some other way to judge the situation. I find that it helps to mirror the words or conversational style of my customers. You have such a short time to build rapport that you need something to separate you from the pack. On the phone, you may have 60 seconds or less to get something going. So, if my customer is loud and brash, I'll try to be the same. If the client talks at a slower pace, I'll slow down, too. If my customer is a little tentative or brusque and self-assured, I'll try to play that back to the customer.

Mirroring may sound like a gimmick, but it's actually an effective way to get on the customer's wavelength so you can move on to the more important parts of the call.

HAVE SOMETHING TO SAY WHEN YOU CALL

Most of your calls may be just a way to stay in touch, but you still should have something to say. For example, if I lose a deal to another salesperson, I'll call the customer a few weeks later and ask how the deal is working out. Is she happy with her salesperson? Is the level of customer service what she expected?

By the way, telephone sales are a particularly good way to stay in touch after you've made an initial face-to-face contact. Customers whom you see in person only once a year will forget all about you unless you call them several times in-between to maintain the relationship. You invest far too much time and effort finding and earning a good client to lose that person to another salesperson just because you didn't stay in touch.

Ralph's Rule: Like any sales tool, the telephone is only as helpful as we make it. Done correctly, telephone sales can boost your productivity to heights you never imagined. Try to have something useful to offer when you call. It will lessen the likelihood of somebody just hanging up on you.

SHADOW A TOP-PRODUCING SALESPERSON

One of the best ways to pick up new sales techniques is to learn from the masters—the top producers in your industry or sales coaches who have acquired numerous techniques and strategies from their own sales careers and from working with other top producers.

The top producers have already blazed the trail. They are well aware of the challenges you face and have probably developed their own strategies for meeting those challenges. They have tips and tricks for overcoming the most common obstacles and taking your sales career to the next level, so you don't have to learn on your own by trial and error.

Most salespeople and other professionals have the mistaken idea that highly successful individuals prefer to keep their "secrets" to themselves. After all, why would they want to help their potential competitors? The fact is that the people at the top usually achieved their success by following in the footsteps of the top producers who preceded them. As a result, they feel an obligation to help others.

This week, I reveal my list of sales mentors (or heroes) and encourage you to identify your own, introduce yourself, and ask them to share their strategies and techniques with you. You're likely to be surprised at just how eager your sales heroes are to become your mentors.

MY SALES MENTORS

Dozens of coaches and mentors have played an instrumental role in helping me to learn my craft and develop the top-producing systems I have relied on throughout my career, including the following:

- Julia Rowland, my grandmother and owner of Fashion Treasure Jewelry—an accomplished saleswoman who embodied the joy of selling.
- Tony and Noel Fox of Fox Brothers Real Estate were the real estate brokers who hired me right out of high school and taught me how important it is to introduce myself to *everyone*. They would drop me off at the local grocery store early in the morning with a stack of business cards and pick me up at night.
- Ira Hayes, the original Ambassador of Enthusiasm, who taught me the power of the word "Great!" A positive mindset is crucial to achieving anything.
- Tom Hopkins, author of *Selling For Dummies* and the guy who wrote the first book of tips for real estate agents.
- Zig Ziglar, the sales superhero, who taught me that if you help enough people get what they want, you will get what you want.
- Charlie "Tremendous" Jones, who revealed to me the life-changing power of people and books. According to Charlie, you are only as good as the people you meet, the books you read, and the audio recordings you listen to.
- Art Fettig, who taught me the difference between a great salesperson and an order taker and who turned me on to the Platinum Rule you'll learn about during Week 44.
- Joe Girard, the top car salesman of all times, who sold cars four miles from where I grew up and took time out of his busy schedule to meet with an up-and-coming salesperson who was willing to learn.
- Floyd Wickman, a real estate agent in my area, who taught me to stay on track and be competent, confident, and natural.

Floyd went on to be and continues to be a successful trainer and speaker.

- Dick Runstatler, my favorite sales manager of all time, who let me be me and taught me how to handle stressful situations. Without Dick's lessons on life, I would be second-guessing every decision I have ever made and will ever make.

- Tom Desmond, a real estate agent I worked with at Earl Keim Real Estate, who was constantly striving to improve himself.

- Earl Keim, a guy who could sell you the house next door, even if you didn't want it. He coined the phrase "Keim Sold Mine."

- Mark Victor Hansen, the "Master of Mindset" and co-creator of *Chicken Soup for the Soul,* who taught me to deflect rejection and continue to pursue my passion.

- Og Mandino (www.ogmandino.com), a humble, yet remarkable man who spent much of his life striving to overcome his own personal challenges and sharing what he discovered through his writing and teaching.

- Tom Antion, the speaker's speaker, who taught me that if you can't talk to people, you can't sell.

- Les Brown, who taught me the power of living with a purpose and who encouraged me to have the willpower to confront even the most daunting challenge.

Tip: If you want to be the best salesperson, hang out with the best salespeople. If you want to be a loving and attentive husband or wife, hang out with loving and attentive husbands or wives. Extend the power of mentoring by seeking out mentors not only in your profession but also to help you navigate your personal life.

IDENTIFY PROSPECTIVE MENTORS

Chances are pretty good that you already know a top producer or sales coach you admire. This could be someone you work with, someone from whom you purchased a product or service, a salesperson you met at a conference or seminar, or even someone who works for the competition.

Unfortunately, most salespeople are reluctant to approach these industry leaders, under the mistaken assumption that these top producers have little time or desire to meet with "lesser" salespeople and reveal their secrets of success. As explained earlier in this chapter, the truth is that the people at the top are often the most generous with their time and with sharing their techniques.

Contact a salesperson you admire and arrange a meeting. Invite the person to lunch or dinner. If you hit it off, ask whether you can shadow the person for a day.

Tip: You can also learn a great deal by mentoring other up-and-coming salespeople who are not as experienced as you. I have discovered that having someone watch me work often motivates me to take my game to the next level. It also forces me to re-think how I do things. In addition, my students often become my teachers, showing me a thing or two.

HIRE A SALES COACH

Another option is to hire a sales coach. Sometimes, you may be too close to your situation to view it objectively. A reputable sales coach can quickly assess the situation, tell you what you're doing right and what you're doing wrong, and offer several suggestions that you can immediately implement.

A good coach may charge you a fee plus expenses for a single day, but if the coach can put you on the path to success, the investment is well worth it.

Ralph's Rule: Success leaves big footprints. By following the trails that others have blazed for you, you can achieve success much sooner and with less effort. You can then head out on your own trails to take your career beyond those who preceded you and leave some big footprints of your own for others to follow.

WEEK 33

TEAM UP WITH A PERSONAL PARTNER

Although you can accomplish a great deal on your own, you can often achieve more, faster by teaming up with someone. This is true whether you have a personal goal (e.g., quit smoking, lose weight, or read more books) or a professional goal, such as expanding your business, beefing up your marketing efforts, or reaching out to new markets.

Salespeople, in particular, often achieve much higher levels of success when they team up with other salespeople to share techniques, practice scripts, challenge one another, and hold one another accountable.

My friend and colleague, Terry Wisner, founder of *Partnering To Success, LLC,* developed his own version of teaming up with a partner, called the *Personal Partnering Process.* Perhaps you already practice personal partnering and aren't even aware of it, or maybe you call it something else, like the *buddy system.*

If you are a member of a group that reads, exercises, or diets together, for example, you are already involved in a basic form of personal partnering. Members of the group set goals together, set deadlines, and meet to share their progress and support one another. Without some peer pressure, you would have a much easier time blowing off whatever goal you set and probably would not make nearly as much progress. The group (or your partner) holds you accountable.

This week, you discover how to team up with a partner to set goals, hold one another accountable, support one another's efforts, and celebrate your achievements on your way to mutual success.

CHOOSE A PARTNER

The first and perhaps most important step in developing a partnership consists of picking the right partner. Teaming up with someone in sales is probably best because another salesperson is likely to be more aware of what you are trying to accomplish and the challenges you are facing. Two salespeople are also more likely to be able to share techniques and strategies. When looking for a partner, try to find someone who:

- Is a salesperson, preferably in the same or a related industry.
- Believes in goal setting and planning.
- Is supportive.
- Is able to offer positive criticism.
- Is at or slightly above your level of success.
- Is someone you like and respect and who likes and respects you.

Avoid partnering with salespeople you may be competing against. You don't want to put yourself in a situation in which you reveal a vulnerability to someone who could potentially use it against you. If you work on a sales team with team members who are mutually supportive, partnering with fellow team members could be the ideal situation.

DEVELOP A PLAN

Things tend not to get done unless they are written down. After you have identified an area for improvement, develop a partnering plan that lays out exactly what you are going to do to achieve your goal. Your plan should include the following:

- *A measurable and realistic goal:* Set a goal that you can measure. "Improve my referral business" is too vague because it fails to specify how you would measure the improvement. "Obtain 30 referrals this month" is a more concrete goal. For more about setting goals, see Week 5.

- *Intermediate goals:* Break down your goal so it does not seem so overwhelming. For example, obtaining one referral per day may seem less daunting than obtaining 30 a month. Your intermediate goals enable you and your partner to check your progress so you can stay on track.

- *Steps you will take to achieve your goal:* Jot down a list of detailed tasks or steps you will take toward achieving your goal. For example, are you going to call existing clients or past clients and ask for referrals? Are you going to ask for a referral each time you make a sale?

- *Deadline:* Write down the date by which you plan on accomplishing your goal. When the date finally arrives, you and your partner can touch base to determine whether you achieved your goal on schedule.

Terry Wisner tells the people he coaches to make sure that their personal partnering plan is *SMART:*

- *Specific:* Provide enough detail to explain how the efforts will culminate in the desired change.

- *Measurable:* Include intermediate goals, so you can track progress.

- *Actionable:* Specify tasks you're going to accomplish and the steps required to complete those tasks.

- *Realistic:* Set realistic objectives, to avoid frustration and disappointment.

- *Timed:* Set deadlines for accomplishing each task and achieving the planned objective.

You and your partners should share your plans with one another to make sure they fulfill all the requirements of a good plan.

Collaborating with your partner every step of the way is the best approach to keeping you both on track.

MEET WITH YOUR PARTNER

Teaming up with a partner requires more than simply stating goals, drawing up a plan, and then heading out on your own. True partners support one another's pursuits and meet regularly to share successes and setbacks, track one another's progress, offer suggestions, and make any necessary adjustments.

The following sections show you how to launch your partnership in the right direction and keep one another on track with regular meetings.

Agree on the Ground Rules

All relationships benefit when all parties involved know what to expect. To start your partnership on the right foot, you and your partner need to agree on a few ground rules, including the following:

- How often you will follow up with one another.
- Method of contact: phone, e-mail, in person, and so forth.
- How you will celebrate your achievements.
- Consequences for not achieving goals.
- Type of support you will offer one another.

Do not feel as though you are responsible for your partner's success. As professionals, each of you is responsible for your own success. You cannot force one another to take specific action, and you should not feel as though you have to. In many ways, you are likely to act as a silent partner; your partner's desire not to let you down is usually sufficient motivation. The role you play is part cheerleader and part facilitator.

Keep Each Other on Track

Weight Watchers has weekly weigh-ins to keep members honest. Part of what motivates each member to stick to his or her plan is that they are well aware of these public weigh-ins. If someone cheats, the scale will tell the truth. This sort of peer pressure is very effective.

Peer pressure is also highly effective in personal partnering. Every time you meet, you naturally want to report to your partner that you have been making progress. As long as you have both clearly stated your primary and intermediate goals, you should be able to tell when one of you is wandering off course.

Consider scheduling meetings frequently at first, say once a week to start. Once you are both on track, you can scale back your meetings to once every two weeks or even once a month. I would not recommend going any longer than a month between meetings.

Review One Another's Performance

Assuming each of you had a plan in place along with a deadline, you should meet on or near the deadline date to review your performance. During this meeting, you and your partner should review your stated goals and how successful each of you was in achieving your goal:

- Did you and your partner meet your goals?
- What did your partner do to assist you?
- What did you do to assist your partner?
- How engaged were you in the partnering process?
- How helpful was the process?
- Could you or your partner have done something different to improve the results next time?
- Were your goals challenging enough? Too challenging?
- What effect did the partnering process have on your success in sales? Can you quantify the value of the process in terms of sales volume or gross revenue?

To make the partnering process most effective, provide each other with honest feedback. This can lead to improvements in the partnering process that can make it more productive next time.

Celebrate Your Mutual Success

You have both met or exceeded your goals. It is now time for the victory dance, or whatever you and your partner choose to do to celebrate your mutual success. Following are some ideas for how you can celebrate together:

- Lunch or dinner at a fine restaurant.
- Shopping spree.
- Trip to the spa.
- Weekend getaway.
- Day at the races or casino.

When partnering improves your sales success, it also boosts your commissions so you don't have to worry too much about the expense.

Ralph's Rule: Partner with people you respect and who respect you, so you will naturally strive to meet or exceed the expectations you have for one another. When you choose the right person, he or she can hold you accountable without having to play the taskmaster.

HOOK UP WITH A MENTOR

M y job is more than my job. It's my passion, my hobby. People say, "What do you do for a hobby?" Well, Saturday and Sunday, even if I'm with my family, I might want to check out a few pieces of real estate just to see what they're like. I think if I sold cars, I'd want to drive around and look at cars. If I sold computers, I'd want to know about all the latest computers. I think the passion, the hobby, comes into play there.

One way to nurture this passion, especially early in your career, is through mentors. A mentor is any person who helps you understand something about yourself and your business. It doesn't have to be a boss necessarily; it can be an inspirational speaker like Zig Ziglar or a relative who showed you the way.

MENTORS IN THE FAMILY

My original mentors were my parents, even though I didn't follow in my dad's footstep as a builder. What I learned from my parents was the importance of having a strong work ethic. My parents would not let me have a paper route because they wanted me to have time for school, but on Saturdays and Sundays, I could go to work for my dad. I'd be there all the time. After he retired, he still worked every single day until he passed away several years ago. I learned from my parents that hard work pays off.

Probably more important than inheriting a strong work ethic, I learned from my parents the importance of doing things for others. My mom would do anything to help someone. I know they helped put people through college and buy cars. I remember my parents would give when they didn't even have it to give. I learned that from them, and today I give a significant part of my time and earnings to charitable affairs. You've got to give something back.

I think I must have gotten my passion for selling from my grandmother. My grandparents came to Detroit from Kentucky in the 1930s so my grandfather could work in the auto industry here. Once, my grandfather got fired for smoking on the job. But, because the auto industry was booming, he was able to get hired at another plant right away. At first, they lived with a few other families in a house in Detroit.

Growing up, my brothers and I were very close with my grandparents. We called them Mom and Dad and we called my parents Mommy and Daddy. It was almost like having two sets of parents. Eventually, my grandparents and my family lived across the street from one another. My grandparents also had some property where they raised ponies. Sometimes, after school, we would go to their house to ride the ponies. Growing up with two sets of parents seemed to us to be the ideal arrangement.

When I was a toddler, my grandmother started a jewelry business. She sold costume jewelry under the name Fashion Treasures. I really enjoyed being at her selling parties—I liked being around all the people.

They tell me stories about how if the phone would ring while I was soaking in the bathtub, I'd jump out of the tub, run down the hallway naked, grab a piece of paper and pencil, say, "It's jewelry business, I'll get it!" There are even some photos of me doing this, naked and wet.

Later in life, I married the person who would become my most intimate mentor and confidante—my wife, Kathleen. Because we love each other dearly, Kathleen does not pull any punches when she offers insights on what I need to do to become a better salesperson . . . or a better person altogether. Having someone who accepts you as you are and still challenges you to become the best you can be is perhaps the most valuable mentor-mentee relationship you can have.

MENTORS IN THE NEIGHBORHOOD

Another mentor I can remember was Frank Gardner. I worked in his gas station after school and eventually took on the role as manager. Frank was just a great guy. I learned how to deal with people from him.

For example, I and another guy who worked there had our girlfriends come over in the summer. It was warm, and we were washing and waxing our cars in the two bays in the gas station. I remember Frank and his wife went out to dinner that night. I didn't think there'd be any problems. If people came in for gas, we'd hurry out and take care of them

Well, I remember Frank pulling up, and from the look on his face I knew he wasn't happy. He came in, took his tie and jacket off. He helped us dry both the cars. Then he asked us to move the cars out, and he asked me to come into his office because I was the one in charge. When we went into his office, Frank asked me, "What do you think you did wrong?"

I said, "We shouldn't have been washing our cars when we were working for you, Frank."

He said, "No, that's not what you did wrong. Sometimes there's nothing to do; you've got all your work done. What you did wrong was you were doing two cars at the same time, and both of my stalls were full. If somebody drove by and wanted an oil change or a tire fixed, they would think I was busy and would go to another station. I don't mind you working on your own vehicles, but at least the customers should know that they could pull up here and you could take care of them."

Well, Frank could have fired me, but he didn't. Instead, he taught me a lesson about business and how to treat people. He could have yelled at me, but the way he corrected me, I learned a lot. It's in me forever.

MENTORS IN YOUR OFFICE

When you hear the word "mentor," you are likely to think of someone in a superior position—a boss, a top-producing salesperson as discussed in Week 32, or an industry leader. However, anyone in any position can function as your mentor. Currently, some of my wisest mentors are the people who work "for" me. I put that in quotes because I never really think of people working *for* me; I think of them working *with* me as my fellow teammates.

My "assistant," Lois Maljak, whom I prefer to call my second in command, is a valuable mentor. We actually tend to mentor one another. Lois often brings me back to reality, constantly reminding me that sales transactions and other business deals are less important than the people involved in those transactions. She also functions as my focus, so I can remain chaotically creative and still attend to the particulars of finishing what we have started.

Look around and try to identify the mentors who surround you. Don't overlook those closest to you who may consider you their role model. You can learn something valuable from everyone you meet.

Ralph's Rule: Mentors come in all varieties, from relatives and friends to bosses and coworkers. If you don't have anyone guiding you right now, make it your business to find at least one person who can teach you something new. You can learn so much from the right people.

JOT DOWN IDEAS FOR NEW OPPORTUNITIES

I'm a big believer in jotting down those random flashes of inspiration we all have. Instead of physically writing anything down, I dictate into my digital recorder, as I described in a previous chapter.

Several years ago, I decided to create a system to involve my whole staff in this process. So I created my "Idea of the Week" book. I've subtitled mine "the greatest success generating tool" because that's what it is. I encouraged all my staff to enter thoughts into it when they get good ideas. Everyone is encouraged to page through it from time to time and adopt and adapt any ideas they find useful.

For example, one month one of my top buyer agents, Paul Corona, wrote this: "Old Idea but Good Idea: Having a great relationship with another agent or two so you have the ultimate in teamwork when you are out of town or need assistance with a client." This ties into my system of referrals and teamwork around the office. We have started a buddy system whereby each new employee partners with someone for a while, not only to learn the ropes but also to have someone to inspire him and watch his back. Paul's idea was a reminder to all of us that lone-wolf salespeople are less successful than those who can team up with others.

This idea has grown into a system for running a team-based real estate office. Recently, I partnered with John Featherston, founder and CEO of RISMedia, to co-author a book titled, *Power Teams: The Complete Guide to Building and Managing a Winning Real Estate Agent Team.* The best ideas have a way of developing into something great, taking on a life of their own, and opening your eyes to new business opportunities.

Sometimes the ideas are just simple little things to make life easier. A couple winters ago someone wrote this: "Get salt spreader fixed and salt entire parking lot instead of shoveling salt." It was a reminder to me to take care of the everyday working conditions around my office.

A couple of years ago this suggestion turned up: "Make a checklist to put into buyer's package when meeting with them, a reminder about insurance, etc." Customers really appreciate any help we give them navigating the details of a transaction, so this was a very useful suggestion.

Another day, an employee reminded me that my "Voice mail message should be upbeat—not regular . . . Need enthusiasm!" You bet I followed up on this one right away!

One winter, our in-house lawyer, Peter Allen, wrote: "Geri to do fax cover sheets for each salesperson/loan officer." Again, this wasn't a giant brainstorm but just a little idea to make us more efficient. Along with all the other ideas we generated, however, it helped us achieve tremendous improvements in efficiency from year to year.

Starting an idea book is as simple as buying a notebook or journal and putting it in a prominent place in the office. Let everyone know they are free to jot down ideas and suggestions. They can sign their names or not as they choose.

One rule you may want to put into action is that all ideas must be constructive. In my office, I have a complaint box with the slot taped over to remind everyone on the team that I don't want to hear complaints. I want to hear solutions and constructive criticism. Complaining alone does not lead to positive change. Challenge your staff to think creatively and share their ideas freely. Nobody should be bashful about expressing an idea.

Ralph's Rule: To achieve continuous improvement, tap into everyone's creativity day-to-day and year-to-year. Creating a system to capture flashes of inspiration will pay enormous dividends.

NURTURE RELATIONSHIPS

It's never about the numbers, the profit and loss statement, or the bottom line . . . it's ALWAYS about the people, and the people only.
— Roberto Giannini, Head Soccer Coach, Wabash College

A funny thing happens when you become a top-producing salesperson. You stop selling. You stop worrying about the numbers—about sales quotas and profits and the bottom line. You start talking to people. You build relationships, partnerships, and business synergies.

You stop *selling*, but you end up with more sales earning far more than you ever did when you were trying to sell.

What's the explanation behind this phenomenon? It is captured in the quote at beginning of this chapter: "it's ALWAYS about the people, and the people only."

FORGET ABOUT THE MONEY

When you achieve a certain level of financial success, when you have money in the bank and no longer have to worry about paying bills, you can afford to focus more energy on people and relationships. And when you do that, sales begin to soar! Your clients and prospective clients, who pretty much consist of everyone you meet, can sense your genuine interest in their lives and their businesses and your commitment to serving their best interests, and they feel more comfortable buying from you than from a salesperson who appears ambitious to the point of being desperate.

If you have not quite achieved the status of top-producing salesperson, I recommend that you stop waiting for the time when you have enough money and do it now. Drop the profit motive. Give up the mentality of bottom-line thinking. Stop worrying so much about sales quotas. Start thinking about the *top line*—the people—and establishing personal relationships with your clients and business contacts.

STOP HUNTING, START FARMING

Salespeople who are constantly hunting for business are constantly disappointed and tend to burn out quickly. If you consider yourself a member of this group, then perhaps you need to stop hunting and start farming. By transforming yourself from hunter into farmer, you change your entire lifestyle. Instead of suffering through feast or famine, you establish a steadier flow of referral business that can keep you well fed throughout the year.

The transition can be quite a challenge, particularly if you've had the hunter's mindset drilled into you from the beginning of your career. The easiest way to conceptualize your new role is to think of yourself less as a salesperson and more as a friend to your clients. In other words, stop selling and start nurturing relationships.

Business consultant and visionary Terry Brock refers to this as R-Commerce (Relationship-Commerce). Instead of focusing your mind and energy on the quantitative aspects of selling, such as gross sales and your bottom line, you focus on the qualitative aspects of selling—building mutually beneficial relationships. This approach requires a significant investment up front, but it pays handsome dividends over time. By establishing productive relationships, you sow the seeds that produce a bumper crop of business for many years to come.

GET CONNECTED

According to my research (at weddings and funerals, class reunions, and family gatherings) everyone knows at least 250 other people. So I view every encounter I have with someone as a chance to connect with 250 others. Establish a personal connection with everyone you meet, including the people at the restaurants you frequent, where you have your car serviced, the grocery store, the gas station... everywhere. You never know where a new source of business or a new idea will come from.

You should also take advantage of these more formal networking opportunities:

- Meet people on the job. Get to know everyone you work with.
- Get involved in professional organizations.
- Join your trade association and take on a leadership role.
- Join a community service organization, such as the Rotary Club, Kiwanis, the Lions Club, or Habitat for Humanity.
- Join the local Chamber of Commerce and attend meetings regularly.

Tip: Opt for soft networking over hard networking. Soft networking is more social and less business-oriented. Follow the age-old advice of "Make friends *before* you need them." And make sure everyone you meet receives your business card.

GATHER CONTACT INFORMATION

Not everyone you meet will buy something from you, but almost everyone you meet can benefit you in some way—perhaps by selling you something you need or steering business in your direction. Start collecting names and other information and building your database.

Whenever you meet someone new, whether you bump into them in person, over the phone, or online, use your sales skills to ask questions and gather the following information about the person:

- Career, work, or major in school.
- Interests and hobbies.
- Goals or dreams.
- Special talents.
- Contact information.
- Birthday, anniversary, and other personal information.

When I return to the office at the end of each day, I scan in all of the business cards I collected and then pass along any additional details to my assistant who types the information into Microsoft Outlook. I don't want to lose any shred of valuable information, so I try to tell the entire story of the person, including where and how we met and everything that person told me.

KEEP IN TOUCH

A relationship is like a bicycle—you have to keep pedaling to keep it moving forward. Maintaining a relationship may not require a great deal of energy, but it does require some regular attention. One of the ways I keep in touch is through my Hour of Power, which I discussed in Week 22. I strongly encourage you to launch your own Hour of Power.

GIVE

When you give people memorable gifts, they tend to remember you as well as the gift. The first gift you should present someone is your business card. For people who already have your business card, I recommend giving them one of the following:

- Your brochure.
- An inspirational book.
- A thank-you card.
- Flowers or candy.
- Good deeds.

You will learn more about giving in Week 44, where I discuss the Platinum Rule.

Ralph's Rule: While making the transition from hunter to farmer, you may still have to hunt to keep some revenue flowing in, but don't forget to start planting, so you can harvest tomorrow's bumper crop.

LAUNCH YOUR OWN BLOG

O ne of the most effective ways to establish a presence on the Internet and build a reputation as an industry expert and trustworthy salesperson is to create and manage your own blog. A blog is an online journal of sorts that you can use to self-publish content on any imaginable topic—from religion and politics to cars, homes, insurance, personal financing, pet care, and anything else.

I have several blogs: FlippingFrenzy.com to raise awareness of real estate and mortgage fraud, ForeclosureSelfDefense.com to inform homeowners facing foreclosure of their options (and promote my book *Foreclosure Self-Defense For Dummies*), AboutRalph.com/blog (to let people know where I'll be speaking, what I am writing, and where I've been quoted in the press), PowerfulSelling.com where I offer additional tips and tricks on how to market and sell more effectively and where I promote my books on selling-related topics.

Blogs have three huge advantages over standard web sites:

1. You can post content on a blog simply by filling out a form and clicking the Publish button. Design templates apply the formatting codes for you, so you don't have to deal with complicated tags that are associated with Web page design.

2. Search engines love blogs. By posting a couple of unique and significant items every week, you can expect to see your blog entries start popping up in search engine results on Google, Yahoo!, MSN, and other search sites.

3. You don't have to create all the content. Blogs encourage visitors to post comments on the articles you post. The more comments your blog entries inspire, the faster your blog grows and the higher its profile becomes with search engines—without you having to do extra work. In addition, the comments feature helps build a community of users around your blog, and we all know that community sells.

Blogs do a much better job than standard web sites at feeding search engines what they're hungry for: fresh, relevant content and links. While you may create a small web site and attract a small amount of traffic, a comparably sized blog can attract thousands of enthusiastic visitors.

BRUSH UP ON BLOG BASICS

Blogs began as a tool for anyone with a computer and a connection to the Internet to create and share their own personal diaries, journals, and commentary, but they soon evolved into sources for freelance news stories and editorial content. People with inside information or strong opinions could publish whatever they were thinking without having to be employed by a newspaper, magazine, radio station, or TV network. Blogging turned the power of the news media over to the people. This is still one of the most popular uses for blogs today.

As with most things on the Internet, businesses eventually started to tap blogging for commercial use. The popularity of blogs combined with their ease of use made them a perfect marketing tool for corporations, and the popularity of corporate blogging started to soar. Now, many businesses that have any sort of Internet presence have corporate blogs in addition to their more static web sites. Even Martha Stewart Living has a blog: blogs1.marthastewart .com!

Understand the Two Main Components

A blog requires two components to exist—a hosting service and blogging platform:

1. The *hosting service* is the computer on the Internet where all the blog's files are stored. When people visit your blog using their Web browsers, they are looking at files stored on the hosting service.

2. The *blogging platform* is the tool you use to create and manage your blog. Think of it as a word processor for blogging. When you log into your blog as its administrator, the platform presents you with a work area where you can type and format a new blog entry, edit or delete comments that visitors have posted, adjust the overall appearance and layout of your blog, and much more.

Add a Style with Design (Presentation) Templates

One of the great things about blogs is that you can easily post content to the Web without having to learn or deal with complicated hypertext markup language (HTML), the codes that control the look and layout of Web pages. Blogging allows you to publish content by typing into a form and then clicking the Publish button.

The HTML and cascading style sheets (CSS) codes are stored in design templates (often called *presentation templates*) that are included with most blogging platforms. The design templates control the look and layout of your blog. You can choose from one-, two-, or three-column templates to apply an overall layout to your blog. These design templates also contain the codes that control fonts, type sizes, and colors; control the appearance of headings, bulleted lists, and numbered lists; and ensure that each page on your blog has a consistent design.

Perhaps the coolest and most convenient aspect of design templates is that you can select a different template or customize the template at any time to change the look and layout of every single page of your blog, without touching the content. Any changes you make are automatically applied to every single page of your blog.

TEST DRIVE A BLOG FOR FREE

To get a feel for blogging before you invest too heavily in it, I recommend that you try one or two of the free blogging platforms currently available. You can set up a free blog on any of the following web sites and take the company's blogging platform for a spin to see what each one has to offer:

- WordPress at wordpress.com.
- Blogger at www.blogger.com.
- Yahoo! 360° at 360.yahoo.com.

Don't spend too much time or effort configuring your blog and posting entries to it. Although most blogging platforms do allow you to export your content so you can set up your blog elsewhere using a different platform, there is no point in wasting time fine-tuning your blog only to have to start over when you set up your permanent blog. In addition to the extra work involved, if you move your blog from one of these free services to its own domain (e.g., moving from yourname.blogspot.com from Blogger to www.yourname.com), search engines may lose track of your posts, and it could take weeks before they get around to re-indexing them.

CHOOSE A BLOG HOST AND PLATFORM

The first step to launching your own blog is to choose a blog host and platform. Although the companies that offer hosting services and platforms are too numerous to cover, your choices can be grouped into the following four categories:

1. *Free, hosted platforms,* like the ones I encouraged you to test drive, offer a cheap and easy way to blog, but probably don't offer the flexibility and power you need for long-term use.
2. *Turnkey solutions* are generally the most expensive, but they deliver all the benefits of a hosted platform along with the flexibility to customize the blog's design and layout and choose your own domain name. An example of a general-purpose turnkey solution is TypePad (typepad.com), which is suitable for both personal and professional blogs. You may also find companies that offer turnkey solutions for specific industries, such as Kinetic Blogs (kineticblogs.com).

3. *Standalone platforms* are for those who want to get their hands dirty and learn blogging from the ground up. You register your own domain name (for about $10 per name per year), subscribe to a hosting services (for about $6 to $10 per month), install the blogging platform, and start blogging. If you choose this route, I recommend that you go through a full-featured hosting service, such as Yahoo! (smallbusiness.yahoo.com/webhosting/), BlueHost (www.bluehost.com), or InMotion (www.inmotionhosting.com). These services can help you register your domain name and install your blogging platform of choice—most blogging platforms are free or charge a small licensing fee.

4. *Remote hosting options* combine the power of a standalone blogging platform with the flexibility of hosting the blog on your own domain. Both Blogger and Typepad offer these options. The blog runs on your domain and hosting service, but you go to Blogger or Typepad to post content and configure your blog. This way, you can avoid the complications of installing the blog on your hosting service. In addition, you always have access to the latest version of the blogging platform without having to upgrade it yourself.

Caution: Avoid the temptation to advertise on your blog. All content should be soft-sell, if you're selling at all. Your primary goal is to establish yourself as a trustworthy subject matter expert. When you achieve this goal, consumers are more likely to buy from you than from a complete stranger.

EARN HIGHER SEARCH ENGINE RANKINGS

As I revealed early in this chapter, one of the most significant benefits that blogs offer is that they attract the attention of search engines, including Google. You don't earn a high search ranking, however, simply by installing a blogging platform and adding a couple of posts. You need to be more proactive than that. Here are some suggestions for giving your blog a higher profile with search engines:

- *Post fresh, relevant content.* You can read about all sorts of clever ways to fool search engines into giving your blog a higher rank, but nothing works better than being real—post relevant articles once or preferably twice a week.

- *Concentrate on key words and phrases.* When composing a post, make sure you use the words and phrases people are likely to search for when looking for the content you are providing.

- *Tag your blog entries:* Many blogging platforms allow you to tag your entries with key words and phrases to make the posts easier to find.

- *Cross-market your web site and blog.* When you blog about something related to your company, insert links in your blog entry to your company web site. Similarly, add a permanent link to your blog from your company's web site navigation bars.

- *Populate your blogroll with relevant listings.* Most blogging systems enable you to create a *blogroll:* a list of other web sites and blogs that are relevant to the content you post on your site. Creating a blogroll serves a dual purpose: It helps search engines determine what your site is about, and it encourages other web site and blog creators to link to your site as a way of thanking you for linking to their sites.

- *Add relevant links to posts.* By adding links to the body of your posts (in addition to the blogroll), you show that your content is part of the community. If you read an article on the Web that you would like to respond to, for example, you can post your response and include a link to the article you are referencing.

- *Add links to cross-reference other posts on your blog.* You may have noticed that when you search on Google, some sites have a double listing—a main listing with a sublisting indented below it. Studies have shown that people click these listings more often than they click single listings displayed in the same list of search results. You're more likely to obtain double listings if your posts contain links that cross-reference other posts on your blog.

- *Register your blog with blog directories.* Some search engines focus exclusively on blogs, but they may need a little help finding your blog. To make sure your blog is included in the search results, consider registering your blog with several blog directories and search engines, including Technorati (www.technorati.com), Google (www.google.com/addurl/), Globe of Blogs (www.globeofblogs.com), Blogarama (www.blogarama.com), Blogflux (www.blogflux.com), and Best of the Web Blog Directory (blogs.botw.org).

- *Contribute to other people's blogs.* Blogging is all about establishing yourself as a credible source, an expert, in the community in which you do business. By contributing to other blogs in the community, you prove that you're dedicated to the community, not just to your own agenda. When posting to other people's blogs, however, it's even more important not to advertise or blatantly try to drive traffic to your blog.

Ralph's Rule: The Internet has transformed the twenty-first-century marketplace into a place where reputation and word-of-mouth advertising are the keys to success. By creating a blog and populating it with fresh, relevant content, you can build trust and create a buzz that sells.

TRY AN INTERNET LEAD GENERATION SERVICE

Throughout this book, I provide advice on how to generate your own leads. If you already have a web site and blog, you're making your 100 phone calls a day, practicing the 10-10-20 technique, and networking with everyone who crosses your path, you should already have more business than you can handle on your own. (Hopefully, you have hired one or more assistants to help you handle the extra business so you don't have to turn customers away.)

If you have the time and resources to take on even more business, then consider subscribing to an Internet lead generation service as a source for additional prospects.

In the real estate industry, lead generation services are a huge industry in and of themselves. Companies including HomeGain (HomeGain.com), HouseValues (HouseValues.com), and Agent-Connect (AgentConnect.com) are only a few companies that gather contact information of people who show an interest in buying or selling a home, screen those leads, and provide them to real estate agents all across the country who subscribe to the service.

While Internet lead generation has pretty much gotten its start in the real estate industry, it has quickly spread to other industries, including banks, insurance companies, and even the medical industry. No matter what you sell, there's probably an Internet lead generation company that can help you track down prospective customers.

ASSESS THE BENEFITS OF LEAD GENERATION SERVICES

Lead generation services offer several benefits to you as a salesperson, including the following:

- *Marketing and advertising:* Lead generation services often have a pre-established Internet presence that draws prospective customers, so you can invest less time and effort establishing yourself on the Internet. Many of these services also pay for search engine advertising, giving them a much higher search engine ranking than you could afford on your own. By relieving the burden of Internet marketing and advertising, lead generation services free your time and resources to follow up with motivated customers rather than having to find them.

- *Screening:* Perhaps the biggest benefit of a high-quality Internet lead generation service is that the service screens out prospects who are less ready, willing, and able to make a purchase decision in the near future. This enables you to concentrate your efforts on highly motivated clients. One of the most important factors in choosing an Internet lead generation service is how well the service screens out poor leads.

- *On-demand leads:* An Internet lead generation service gathers leads 24/7, so you can focus on more important tasks, such as serving your clients. When you need more leads, the service can supply them on demand.

Tip: When you are in the market for an Internet lead generation service, find out how many salespeople receive the same leads, the average age of the leads, and what the company does to screen out less promising leads. Many companies promote their services by boasting about the total number of leads, but if 20 salespeople in your market are receiving the same leads or if the leads are old or bogus (visitors entered fake information to register on the site with no intention of being contacted), then you could end up paying for bad leads that merely waste your time.

BE PREPARED

I was once the official spokesperson for a promising Internet lead generation service for real estate agents. Part of my job was to provide training to real estate agents, so they could make optimum use of the high-quality leads the service sent them.

The biggest problem we encountered is that many of the agents who subscribed to the service were ill-prepared to follow up on the leads they received. They would receive leads and simply sit on them until they "had some free time." By the time they got around to contacting the hot lead, it had gone cold or another agent already snapped it up.

To maximize the return on your investment, you need to put a lead-management system in place before you even subscribe to a service. Your lead-management system should do the following:

- *Qualify the leads.* Rank your prospects A, B, and C. Focus your sales efforts on the A-level prospects, but don't ignore the Bs and Cs. You may be able to convert them into A-level prospects later. In Week 39, I show you how to date your leads.

- *Be the first to call.* Clients, especially those who shop on the Internet, demand instant gratification. Even slight delays can result in lost opportunities.

- *Offer the best service.* Chances are pretty good that the same lead has been distributed to several salespeople in your market. When you contact the lead, you had better be in a position to offer superior service.

- *Treat your lead like a customer.* Too many salespeople expect leads to be willing buyers. You still have to sell. Treat the prospect well, and you can turn the prospect into a customer. Continue to follow up, so that the person becomes a customer for life.

Ralph's Rule: Lead generation systems are not perfect, but they do provide another source for contacting prospective customers. The more proactive you are at following up on the leads you receive, the more business the service will generate for you.

DATE YOUR LEADS . . . OR SOMEONE ELSE WILL

P eople who know me are rarely aware that I moonlight as a marriage counselor. I tell workaholic spouses that they had better "Date your wife (or husband) or someone else will." The same can be said to salespeople: Date your leads or someone else will.

I see far too many agents buy leads and then completely drop the ball on nurturing those leads. This is the equivalent of discovering your soul mate and doing absolutely nothing to get that person to marry you; you don't flirt with the person, send a card or gift, or even ask the person out on a date. When you receive a lead, even if it's only lukewarm, you must continue to nurture that lead until the person finally decides to hire you or buy from you.

CREATE A SYSTEM

Before you even think about signing up with a lead generation service (as I mentioned briefly during Week 38), you should have a system in place for managing leads. Your system should cover the following:

- *Filtering leads:* Although your lead-generation service may filter out all but the most promising leads, you probably want to do your own filtering, so you can focus your energy on leads that you have a better chance of converting into sales.

- *Making initial contact:* Being the first to call is a key step in converting leads into sales, so make sure you have a system in place that enables you or someone on your team to contact the prospect within an hour of receiving the lead. You have to beat your competition to the punch.

- *Gathering information:* Create a form to fill out or a script that enables you to gather the information you need to effectively sell to each prospect. Remember, your first step in the sales process is to ask questions—you can't sell if you don't know what your customer wants.

- *Following up:* Some prospects may require several months to make a purchase decision. Your system should provide a way to remain in contact with prospects during this time, via phone, e-mail, paper mail, or some other method. A follow-up method that's automated is usually best because it requires less of your time. Whenever I receive a new lead, I add the person to my drip e-mail campaign, as discussed later in this chapter.

BE THE FIRST TO CALL

The nurturing process commences as soon as you receive the lead. In most cases, you are not the only salesperson receiving the lead. Your lead generation service probably sent the lead to several other salespeople in your area, and the first person to contact the lead has the best chance, by far, of ultimately landing the sale.

You should have a system that enables you to check incoming leads wherever you may be. Some lead generation services can notify you of leads via e-mail and forward them to your cell phone or wireless communications device at the same time. Even if you are out making sales calls, you can check for incoming leads and contact prospects immediately. Any hesitation can undermine future efforts.

WORK ON YOUR FOLLOW-THROUGH

After that first contact, keep in touch with your lead. One of the best ways to do this is to add the person to a *drip e-mail* campaign. With drip e-mail, a series of messages are sent out automatically once every week or so, so the person does not have the opportunity to forget about you.

When the prospect eventually decides to buy, he or she can quickly open your e-mail message to obtain your contact information and call or e-mail you to obtain more information or purchase whatever it is you are selling. You can set up a drip e-mail campaign online at any of several drip e-mail management sites. I use Rainmaker E-Central at www.rainmakerecentral.com.

At the same time, you should mail a marketing packet to your prospective client. Your packet should include a folder with the following materials:

- Your business card.
- A letter of introduction describing who you are and how you help your clients.
- Your resume.
- Your company, team, or personal mission statement.
- A brochure.
- Reprints of any positive press you received in the newspapers.

Remember, your marketing packet represents you, so invest in an attractive design and layout. To establish a brand presence in the mind of the person receiving the packet, every item in your marketing packet should have a consistent look and feel. For a refresher course on marketing, skip back to Week 17.

BE PERSISTENT

If you do not hear back from your lead, call the person sooner rather than later. Ask the person where he or she is in the decision process and whether you can do anything right now to assist them.

Whatever you do, do not let that lead off the hook. Before my wife agreed to marry me, I had to ask her 11 times! Some leads can be just as picky when choosing a salesperson to buy from.

Remain persistent without nagging, and transform those leads into commissions.

DATE YOUR CLIENTS, TOO

Your best leads come from your best clients, so be sure to date your best clients, too. This doesn't mean selling to them every chance you get. It means establishing a long-term relationship, so that when they or someone they know needs whatever you are selling, they think of you first.

Every month or so, touch base with past clients. Send a letter, an e-mail message, or a newsletter; call them on the phone; send them a card or present on their birthday or anniversary. Whatever you do, don't sell. Just let them know that you're thinking about them, so they will think about you. One of the best ways to keep in touch is by making phone calls, as discussed during Week 22.

Ralph's Rule: Date your leads... or someone else will. It's highly unlikely that you are the only salesperson in your market offering the products or services you carry. To win over your leads, you need to be the most attentive suitor.

BUILD TRUST IN ONLINE COMMUNITIES

W hen marketing and selling products online, trust is an all-important commodity. Studies consistently show that consumers will pay a little extra on Amazon.com and other established retail outlets for the peace of mind of placing orders with companies that have a proven track record of security and customer service. Likewise, eBay sellers who have lots of positive buyer feedback have a huge advantage in the marketplace over sellers who are just starting out. The fact is that trust sells.

Another fact is that consumers talk. They talk about products, services, companies, and even individual salespeople and merchants. They post product reviews. They expose scams and incompetence. They rail about defective products and companies that over-promise and under-deliver. And they sing the praises for top-notch products and services and the people who sell them. Consumers who share common interests also form their own communities where they share information.

With the assistance of a computer and an Internet connection, consumers can log onto the Internet at any time of day or night and check out what their peers have to say on social media sites, like FaceBook, MySpace, LinkedIn, YouTube, and Second Life. They can instantly connect with one another using instant messaging programs. They can even vote on the content they like or dislike, rate businesses and products, and much more.

Through a host of technologies including social networking sites, discussion forums, and blogs, consumers create their own social media that empowers consumers to market and advertise products and services to one another. Consumers can generate either positive or negative press for you and what you sell, depending on how you present yourself online and on the quality of products and services you provide.

In this chapter, you will discover the various forms of social media, examine some of their benefits and drawbacks, and learn techniques for attracting positive press from consumer-advertisers.

WHAT CONSTITUTES SOCIAL MEDIA?

Social media is a term that loosely defines a collection of tools and technologies that enables Internet users to create and publish their own user-generated content. Developers are constantly releasing new tools and technologies, so any list of social media is destined to be out of date by the time it's published, but during the writing of this book, social media encompassed the following:

- *Discussion forums* (often referred to as message boards, bulletin boards, or newsgroups) have been around much longer than most other types of social media sites. They cover every topic imaginable, from caring for your car to training your dog (or cat) to knitting socks.

- *Blogs*, as discussed during Week 37, enable anyone with a computer and an Internet connection to publish their own thoughts, insights, and opinions.

- *Collaborative information sites* encourage users to contribute content. Wikipedia (www.wikipedia.com), for example, offers an online encyclopedia composed by Internet users. Users can even create their own mini-encyclopedias, called *wikis*, which can remain independent from or tie into Wikipedia.

- *Social news* sites allow users to post their own news stories and vote and comment on stories others have posted. Social news sites include Digg (www.digg.com), StumbledUpon (www.stumbledupon.com), Reddit (www.reddit.com), Shoutwire (www.shoutwire.com), and Bringr (www.bringr.com).

- *Photo sharing* sites allow you to upload photographs, and comment and vote on other people's photographs. Popular photo-sharing sites include Flickr (www.flickr.com), Photobucket (www.photobucket.com), Picasa (picasa.google.com), and SnapFish (www.snapfish.com).

- *Video sharing* is becoming more and more popular as individuals and businesses of all sizes produce their own short clips and post them on the Web. By far the most popular video-sharing site as I was writing this book was Google's YouTube (www.youtube.com). Other such sites include LiveLeak (www.liveleak.com), Metacafe (www.metacafe.com), Jumpcut (www.jumpcut.com), Grouper (www.grouper.com), and VideoEgg (www.videoegg.com).

- *Social networks* enable people with shared interests to connect with one another and hang out online. Some of the more traditional and generic social networks include MySpace (www.myspace.com), FaceBook (www.facebook.com), and Friendster (www.friendster.com). Some social networks, like LinkedIn (www.linkedin.com) and Plaxo (www.plaxo.com), provide professional networking opportunities for advancing (or changing) one's career. More and more companies are launching their own social networks, such as Disney XD (disney.go.com/dxd/) and Toyota Prius (www.toyota.com/hybrids/).

- *Q&A networks* bring consumers into contact with experts who can answer their questions in different subject areas. Anyone can post a question. As answers stream in, users can vote on the answer they think is best. Some of the most popular Q&A networks are Answers.com (www.answers.com), Yahoo! Answers (answers.yahoo.com), Askville (askville.amazon.com), and Questionville (questionville.com).

- *Bookmarking* tools enable you to tag Web pages and stories that you think are most important. Bookmarking sites can also estimate the popularity of certain content based on the number of people who have bookmarked it. The most popular bookmarking site, as I was writing this book, was de.licio.us (de.licio.us). Other sites in this category include Diigo (www.diigo.com), TekTag (www.tektag.com), and Spurl (www.spurl.net).

Every type of social media provides you with an opportunity to present yourself and your products and services to dynamic communities and individuals who may be interested in them. The challenge is to present what you have to offer in a way that appeals to the community. This usually means that you need to take a soft-sell approach, if you choose to advertise or sell at all.

Caution: Social media can make or break a company or an individual retailer or salesperson. If the social media turn against you for any reason, they can destroy your business overnight because word spreads almost instantly across the country or around the world. This is not necessarily a bad thing. It simply challenges you to be your best, act with integrity, and be careful of what you post and how you treat your clients.

TAP THE POWER OF SOCIAL MEDIA MARKETING

Whether or not you become actively involved in social media marketing, your clientele or prospective clients are likely to be talking about you or the products and services you sell. They will also be searching for information about what you sell and perhaps looking for a supplier of those products or services.

To use social media marketing to your advantage, I suggest that you take one or more of the following steps:

- *Find out what people are saying about you.* Use your favorite Internet search tool to find out what people have to say about you, the company you work for, the products and services you sell, and your competition. Use Google to search the Web, News, Blogs, and Groups for your name and Company name. Find out what consumers like, dislike, and are looking for but not finding.

- *Identify yourself.* Before customers will buy from you, they will want to know a little bit about you, so provide some information about yourself. You can do this by creating an About Me page on your blog or web site. Create a profile on social networking sites, including LinkedIn, MySpace, and FaceBook. If your industry has its own networking site, such as ActiveRain (www.activerain.com) for real estate professionals, post your profile there. Wherever clients or potential clients tend to hang out and where the service allows you to post your profile or resume, do it. You can find me at www.AboutRalph.com, www.myspace.com/ralphroberts/, activerain.com/blogs/ralphroberts/, www.linkedin.com/in/ralphroberts/, and several other social networking sites, in addition to my own web sites and blogs.

- *Get connected with influential people.* In the world of social media, communities often assess your trustworthiness by the company you keep. If influential people in the community give you a positive recommendation, others in the community are more likely to buy from you.

- *Interact with your clientele.* Look for ways to engage your clientele directly online via message boards, blogs, Q&A sites, and other social media venues. You may even want to include an e-mail form on your web site and blog, so consumers can contact you directly with questions.

- *Meet your clientele face to face.* Seek out opportunities to engage with clients offline. One of the goals of social media is to allow people with similar interests to locate one another in order to set up face-to-face meetings. You might consider scheduling a get-together, seminar, or workshop that enables your online connections to gather and gives you the opportunity to meet prospective clients in person. To schedule and promote face-to-face meetings with likeminded professionals, use Meetup (www.meetup.com).

Remember that social media marketing is all about transforming customers into marketers and advertisers. This requires a concerted effort on your part, both online and offline, to deliver valuable information, insight, products, services, and customer service, so all of your customers will have only good things to say about you.

Social media isn't just about creating marketing buzz or hyping a product; it's about serving your clients with integrity and learning as much as possible about your own business in the process.

Ralph's Rule: Be real. Social media is all about transparency—exposing the truth, however painful it may be. If you make a mistake, never try to cover it up or dodge the truth. Admit your errors, apologize, make it right, and then move on. As long as you are genuine, people will be forgiving. If you try to pull the wool over people's eyes, expect to be tarred and feathered.

FIRE YOUR WORST CLIENTS

W hen you're struggling to do deals in a competitive marketplace, you may think you could never afford to "fire" customers. Letting go of a deal voluntarily seems crazy. After all, when leads are scarce, you want to believe that each of those leads has the potential of turning to gold. Sometimes, though, you have to say "no" to deals, regardless of how desperate you may be for the business. In fact, turning down a deal that's wrong for you may be one of the best skills you learn from this book.

Let me give you an example from my own business. I had a listing that needed a price reduction. (A *listing* is the contract between seller and agent that lets the salesperson represent the home for a given amount of time.) The home was listed at $159,000, and I knew that the price needed to be reduced to about $139,000 in order to sell. The homeowner resisted the price reduction. Making things worse was interference from another agent who was telling my customer that the listing price should have been even higher than $159,000. We argued with the owner for three days. We had a six-month listing agreement, and we were two months into it. I knew this house wasn't going to sell in that market at the higher price.

I figured I'd rather give up the listing today than disappoint the owner four months down the line. So that's what I did. I thanked the customer for the business, but told him I thought another agent would be a better match for him. I walked away and didn't look back. Maybe that other agent was able to sell that house for $159,000. I doubt it, but I was already focused on my other clients who were following my guidance.

I wish I could take credit for this particular tip, but I learned it years ago from my wife, Kathy. She told me I was spending far too much time on certain deals. She'd say, "Ralph, you've spent 10 hours on this file this month. Wouldn't it make sense to take that same time, go out and get five more listings, and let this one go?" And she was right. Part of being a successful salesperson is recognizing which deals to concentrate on and which to let go.

Here's my advice: If you have five deals that you're working, figure out which one gives you the most trouble and let that one go. You will automatically get more business because now you will be able to work more productively instead of spinning your wheels. You can play offense instead of defense.

Having a customer with unrealistic demands is just one reason to make the painful decision to give a customer the heave-ho. In the following sections, I highlight several more.

WHEN YOU CAN'T DELIVER

Sometimes you may not have the product the customer needs, or you're stretched too thin. In these cases, you may be tempted to keep the deal anyway, but remember the downside. If you can't deliver on your promises, you've lost that customer permanently. Even worse, the bad reputation you may get in your industry will hamper all your future efforts. When you can't deliver, drop the deal. Making promises you can't keep is a sure way to destroy your reputation.

WHEN THE CUSTOMER IS TOO NEGATIVE

The old saying about the customer always being right doesn't mean you have to put up with abusive comments or an extremely negative environment. Sometimes a customer distrusts salespeople from the get-go. He may have had a bad experience with a salesperson and he's going to take it out on you.

When you find yourself dealing with a negative, abusive customer, evaluate how important this deal is to you. Obviously, if your production level is high, it's easier to walk away from a deal that's draining your energy. But even if you're struggling to get started, it may be right to drop someone who is consistently abusive or argumentative. After all, you're there to help people, not make enemies. For every nasty customer, there are dozens more nice people who can use your services.

WHEN THE DEAL DOESN'T FIT YOUR BUSINESS PLAN

In Week 6, I encouraged you to draw up your own business plan, and I hope you took my advice. This is a crucial first step on your road to sales success. When I put my plan together, I was very specific about what kinds of deals I was going to do and where I was going to concentrate my efforts. If I find myself getting drawn into a deal that doesn't fit my plan, or one that I know will only distract me from my longer-term goals, I turn it down.

To take a simple example, let's say you've been selling in the lower price range of your industry. Your goal is to move into a higher price range. You should concentrate on developing customers in the higher price range. You'll still get calls from your old marketplace, but you'll have to decide when to let those go to free you to pursue your new goals.

Ralph's Rule: Turning down business may sound like insanity to a struggling salesperson, but knowing when to say "no" and then having the courage to say it is vital to your long-term survival and success. Once you develop a strong customer base, try to develop some judgment about which deals to keep and which to let go. It'll pay off for you in the long run.

ATTEND A CONVENTION OR SEMINAR

Fifty years ago, teachers were not required to take continuing education courses. History teachers were expected to keep up with current events, but English, math, science, foreign language, technology, and the learning styles of students did not change at such a dramatic rate back then as they do now. Now, almost all teachers are required to take continuing education courses to retain their licenses and stay current with ever-accelerating change.

The same is true in most industries, including real estate. Back when I started out, all a real estate agent needed to be successful was a phone, a car, mastery of basic arithmetic, and a strong desire to deliver top-notch customer service. Now, you need all that and more. You need to know your way around a computer and the Internet. You need to know how to use a host of software packages, including e-mail, contact management software, a word processor, spreadsheets, and specialized real estate software, along with Internet-based tools including blogging platforms and instant messaging. And because real estate and mortgage fraud is on the rise, you need to know how to spot it and stop it, so you can protect your clients.

It's very likely that whatever industry you're in, whatever you sell, *how you sell* and *how you service your clients* has been completely revolutionized over the past 10 years and is ever changing. The salespeople who stay on top of these changes and adopt the new methods and technologies are the first to capitalize on these changes. To stay on top, you need to continually seek out educational opportunities.

I LEARNED THE HARD WAY

I used to thumb my nose at education courses for salespeople, thinking that I already knew it all. I used to avoid real estate conventions because I falsely assumed they had nothing to offer. I was completely ignorant of all the networking opportunities, seminars, and workshops available at these industry-wide meetings.

I spent about 20 years selling before I ever considered creating a business plan. I thought I didn't need one because I was already doing 300 transactions a year. Then my friend Stanley Mills helped me draw up my first business plan, which I've followed faithfully. And you know what? With a business plan in place, I was able to double my production to 600 transactions a year.

I am living proof that the greatest mistake of all is arrogance—an inner conviction that you already know just about everything worth knowing. Maybe I'll never be humble—it would be hard to be in my business and not have a pretty healthy ego. But at least now I'm smart enough to listen to others, to profit by listening to them, and to realize that no matter how smart or successful I get, I'll always have a lot to learn.

MY FIRST CONVENTION

About 19 years ago, I decided to go to the National Association of Realtors convention. I have to confess that the only reason I went was so I could write off a trip to San Francisco. My wife, Kathy, always wanted to visit San Francisco, and I figured this would be a golden opportunity. I really had no intention of attending the actual convention. However, when I got there, I decided to have a quick look—to see at what was going on inside the convention hall.

The strangest thing happened. I absolutely fell in love with the speakers. I fell in love with the convention floor. What an amazing place to get ideas. At the time, I had to wonder why, from about 800,000 real estate agents in the nation, only 25,000 bothered to show up. I thought, Wow, all these great speakers, all these great ideas. Where's everybody else?

ATTEND SEMINARS AND WORKSHOPS

A funny thing happens when you reach the pinnacle of your career—when you have achieved a level of success beyond your dreams—you want to do something else. Gertrude Stein once said, "If it can be done, why do it?" You develop a "Been there, done that" mentality and are ready for a new challenge. For many top-producing salespeople, the obvious next challenge is to teach others how to be successful.

Fortunately for up and coming salespeople, when these top-producing salespeople decide to turn their focus on teaching others, they offer their services via industry-related seminars and work-shops. Here, you have the opportunity not only to learn the tricks of the trade from the best of the best, but you actually have a chance to meet some of the heroes of your industry and establish long-term relationships with experts who've proven themselves in the field.

Seminars and workshops also bring you into contact with the most eager students in your industry—those who are dedicated to learning their craft. In other words, you have the opportunity to surround yourself with the most positive individuals in your industry, something I encouraged you to do during Week 4.

NETWORK

Conventions are not only valuable for the learning opportunities they offer but also, and perhaps primarily, for the networking op-portunities. Conventions attract the best of the best and provide you with a chance to establish relationships that continue paying dividends long after everyone clears out of the conference hall.

When I attend conferences, I commonly station myself in the lobby where convention traffic is moderate to heavy and I min-gle. I introduce myself to everyone, touch base with colleagues I've known for years, and get to know people I am meeting for the first time. I hand out my business card and collect cards from everyone. You never know where a new idea or a new partnership will be born.

Ralph's Rule: Attend at least one annual convention in your industry or take at least one continuing education course in your field every year. Education should never stop. Make it part of your annual business plan to enhance your credentials in this way. Again, you ought to be attending shorter seminars all through the year, but at least once annually you should take advantage of a major educational opportunity.

WEEK 43

HOST A SEMINAR OR WORKSHOP

O ne of the secrets to selling in the twenty-first-century marketplace is this: Give away information to sell products and services. It was not always this way, especially in my industry—residential real estate. When I started selling real estate over 30 years ago, real estate agents were the gatekeepers to the information. We had the multiple listing service (MLS), which contained information about all the homes in the area currently for sale. If buyers or sellers wanted access to this information, they had to hire an agent. Now, buyers and sellers can easily pull up listings and perform other housing market research on the Internet.

The agents who are thriving in the new marketplace are the ones who have embraced the change and are providing valuable information to buyers and sellers—information about neighborhoods, local schools, job opportunities in the area, tips on buying and selling a home, and much more. By giving away the information, these agents earn trust and build a strong reputation as marketplace experts. When visitors to their sites need help buying or selling a home, they hire the agent who's been most helpful—the agent who provided them the most valuable information.

I did the same thing early in my career with For Sale by Owner (FSBO) sellers. Most agents refused to show homes that were FSBOs because they thought the sellers were trying to cut them out of their commissions. I took a different approach. I published a book on how to sell your own home and put together an FSBO kit. When I saw a For Sale by Owner sign go up, I stopped at the house, introduced myself to the owners, offered them a free FSBO kit, and wished them luck. I knew that a good percentage of FSBO sellers would ultimately become frustrated trying to sell the home themselves and would need an agent to list it. Whom do you think they called—the agent who refused to show their home or the guy who offered them assistance?

Another way to provide assistance to prospects in your market is to host a free education seminar or workshop.

CASE STUDY: FORECLOSURE SELF-DEFENSE SEMINAR

When my co-authors and I wrote *Foreclosure Self-Defense For Dummies,* we began brainstorming ideas on how to most effectively promote the book. One idea we found most attractive was to put together a free Foreclosure Self-Defense Workshop kit for real estate professionals all across the country. The kit would include a PowerPoint presentation explaining the many options open to homeowners facing foreclosure, tip sheets, an agenda, a sample press release, an e-mail announcement, a promotional flyer, and contact information for ordering copies of *Foreclosure Self-Defense For Dummies* in bulk from the publisher.

Our idea is that we would create a win-win-win situation. Real estate professionals are always looking for ways to give their businesses a higher profile in the community; what better way than to help homeowners who are facing a potentially devastating foreclosure? In the process of staging the workshop, they would be promoting our book. We would create our own mini-sales team. In addition, homeowners facing foreclosure would be the big winners, obtaining free advice on how to avoid foreclosure or at least make a graceful exit without losing everything, including their credit.

During the writing of this book, we were still in the process of getting this somewhat complicated undertaking off the ground, but I am convinced that when we do, it will be a huge success.

IDENTIFY A NEED IN THE MARKETPLACE

Take a lesson from one industry that has mastered the strategy of using workshops to win customers—building supply stores, including Lowe's. Lowe's sells tools, hardware, and supplies for the homeowner do-it-yourselfer, but Lowe's knows that nobody is going to do-it-themselves if they don't know how to do it. They create customers by showing people how to do everything from painting rooms to tiling their bathrooms and handling minor plumbing repairs.

The first step you must take is to identify a need in your community. If you're a financial advisor, for example, people in your marketplace may need information on retirement or estate planning. If you sell insurance, prospective clients may need a basic primer on the different types of life insurance, including term, permanent, whole life, and universal. If you sell automobile parts and supplies (or even cars), consider giving a free workshop on basic auto maintenance. Jewelers could even give seminars on how to shop for and identify the quality of diamonds and other valuable stones.

Use your imagination and brainstorm with your staff to identify several needs for information in your marketplace and then rank the items from greatest to least need. This should give you at least three or four ideas to pursue.

CREATE YOUR WORKSHOP OR SEMINAR

Because you are what I like to call a *content expert*, developing a one- to three-hour seminar or workshop in your area of expertise should be a cakewalk. The biggest challenge you're likely to face is limiting the seminar or workshop to an amount of time that attendees are likely to retain interest.

When planning your workshop or seminar, be sure it includes the following items:

- *Agenda:* A workshop or seminar should follow an agenda, just like a meeting. List the key points you want to cover and estimate the amount of time you plan to spend on each point. Leave some room for questions at the end.

- *Presentation:* In most cases, a PowerPoint presentation is sufficient, but a workshop or seminar can also include demonstrations, hands-on activities, quizzes, and other activities.

- *Audience handouts:* Attendees should walk away from the presentation with valuable materials that reinforce the lessons learned and cause the attendees to remember you. These can include an outline of the presentation, printouts of your PowerPoint slides, tip sheets, and other items.
- *Sign-in sheet:* Use this opportunity to gather contact information for attendees. Before you begin your presentation, pass around a sign-in sheet that asks each attendee for his or her name, address, phone number, and e-mail address.
- *Business cards:* Have a sufficient supply of business cards on hand and make sure every attendee gets one.

PROMOTE YOUR WORKSHOP OR SEMINAR

To ensure that your workshop or seminar is a success, you need to draw a crowd and make sure the local media know about it, so they can give you some (free) positive PR. Here are some ideas on how to promote your workshop or seminar:

- Post an announcement, including the location, date, and time on all of your web sites and blogs.
- Do an e-mail blast announcing the event to everyone in your e-mail address book. Encourage recipients to spread the word.
- Write a press release announcing and describing the event (include the date, time, and location), and make sure every media outlet in your market receives a copy.
- Design a flyer announcing the event and hang it in prominent locations where prospective clients are likely to see it.

Invite the local media to attend the event, as well, so you can generate some post-event PR through news stories and reports in the local media.

Ralph's Rule: Give away information to sell your product or service. When you establish yourself as the leading expert in your field or industry, you become the go-to guy or gal when clients are in the market for whatever you sell.

MASTER THE PLATINUM RULE

C ountless sales gurus recommend the strategy of *giving to get*. In a way, I recommended the same strategy in Week 43, telling you to give away information to get sales. The giving-to-get strategy, however, has one major drawback—it creates an expectation in you that you will get something in return. If that expectation is not fulfilled, it's likely to lead to disappointment and perhaps even make you bitter. In the long run, it could hurt sales—nobody wants to buy from a bitter, grumpy old salesperson.

My friend and colleague Art Fettig offers a more positive approach to giving. In his book *The Platinum Rule*, Art suggests that you give for the sheer privilege of giving. You pay it forward with no expectations of receiving anything in return. The best way to illustrate the rule is to look back at giving experiences you've had.

Think back to the last time you gave or loaned someone money or something else with the understanding that someday that person would return what you gave or repay you in some way and never did. Chances are pretty good that over time your relationship with that person became strained. You may have avoided the person because you didn't know what to say and felt uncomfortable bringing up the issue and clearing the air. Unbeknownst to you, the other person probably felt even worse than you did. Instead of resolving the issue, the relationship simply dissolved. What a tragedy. Giving actually ruined the relationship.

To avoid the ugliness that often results from giving and lending, Art recommends the Platinum Rule—give without expectations. The next time you give somebody something and that person says he'll pay you back, say, "Here's how you can repay me—never try to repay me. Instead, help someone else someday." The next thing you tell him is, "Please don't ever bring this up again. Consider the matter closed. I'm not going to say anything about it, and I don't want you telling anyone about it."

Shortly after I read *The Platinum Rule*, I called Art Fettig, and we struck up a conversation that led to a friendship that has lasted all these years. I started practicing the Platinum Rule, and the more I did, the more confused I became. I called Art and said, "I'm following your advice. I'm telling people not to tell others what I did for them, and they're telling people all sorts of good stuff about me anyway."

Art replied, "Of course, that's what happens with the Platinum Rule. There's nothing you can do about it. You can tell people not to say anything to anyone, but they're going to do it anyway. They're going to say great things about you for the rest of your life. And now they're going to do something nice for another person in need."

I still catch myself giving to get at times, but the more I practice the Platinum Rule, the more it becomes second nature and the less I expect in return. My life has been full of blessings, the most valuable of which are usually the unexpected good things that come my way and people I have the honor of meeting. I still find that unmet expectations almost always cause misery, and I have to remind myself to let those expectations go and follow the Platinum Rule.

Ralph's Rule: Pay it forward. Start living by the Platinum Rule, and make the world a better place.

EXPAND INTO MULTICULTURAL MARKETS

According to the Selig Center for Economic Growth, total purchases by Hispanics, African Americans, Asians, and Native Americans in the United States already exceeds $2 trillion annually. That's bigger than all but the nine largest economies in the world and is expected to rise to $3 trillion by the year 2011.

That's a lot of money. Yet, many salespeople completely ignore customers from other cultures or even unintentionally drive them away through their insensitivity to the differences in other cultures.

During the writing of this book, I was also in the process of co-authoring another book titled *Cross-Cultural Selling For Dummies* with my friend and colleague, cross-cultural selling expert Michael Soon Lee, founder and proprietor of EthnoConnect (www.EthnoConnect.com). Lee, who coined the concept of the Global Rule™ trains salespeople and other professionals on how to accommodate the needs of customers from other cultures. According to the Global Rule, the best strategy to follow is to *treat others as they would like to be treated.*

In this chapter, I reveal some of the most valuable lessons I have learned from Michael Soon Lee and from my experiences in selling to people who come from different racial and ethnic backgrounds.

TEST YOUR CROSS-CULTURAL COMPETENCY

On Lee's web site, www.EthnoConnect.com, you can access several online quizzes that test your cross-cultural competency. As a first step, I encourage you to visit the site, click the Take a Quiz link, click the link for taking the Salesperson Cultural Competence Quiz, and spend some time answering the questions.

When you are finished, your quiz is graded and you receive your score. You'll then have a pretty good idea of whether you need to read our book on cross-cultural selling or sign up for one of Lee's seminars.

Tip: Lee points out that one of the most common mistakes salespeople make is that they try to "treat everyone the same." Certainly, you want to provide fair and equal treatment for everyone, but treating everyone the same does not account for cultural differences. You need to treat everyone the way they want to be treated.

FOLLOW YOUR CUSTOMER'S LEAD

Ever since I can remember, I have practiced *mirroring*. I carefully observe how my customers act and talk, and I try to behave more like them to make them feel more comfortable with me. If I meet with a couple who are somewhat reserved, I tend to rein in my gestures and speak a little more softly. If one of my clients speaks fast and loud and is highly animated, I do the same.

According to Lee, mirroring is even more important when selling to customers from other cultures. For many Asians, for example, direct eye contact can be very uncomfortable, yet some salespeople will try to force eye contact by leaning down to place their face in the customer's line of sight. In addition, every culture has its own comfort zone—personal space that may be greater or less than what Americans find comfortable. Middle Easterners tend to be close talkers, whereas people from Germany, Switzerland, and Japan prefer to stand farther away.

Lee recommends letting the customer establish a comfortable distance and set the tone for your greeting and meeting. If the customer reaches out to shake your hand, shake his or her hand. If the person embraces you, hug the person back. If he bows, return the bow. If the person steps closer to you, hold your ground instead of stepping back. By following the customer's lead, you can generally do no wrong.

TAKE A COMPREHENSIVE APPROACH

One of the most important lessons that Lee teaches is that cross-cultural marketing, advertising, and sales is not enough to win over customers from other cultures. Your business must make an effort at every level to appeal to customers from other cultures.

Lee tells the story of a pizzeria that decided it wanted a slice of the multicultural marketplace, so it started running advertisements in the language of the people it was trying to attract. Unfortunately, nobody on staff spoke the language, so when these customers started calling in, nobody could take the order. This approach was actually counterproductive, causing ill will in the community that the pizzeria was trying to attract.

To appeal to customers from other cultures, make sure you make adjustments in the following departments:

- *Marketing and advertising:* Include images of the people you are trying to attract in your advertisements. In addition, modify your advertisements to address the values and needs of the target group. For example, many new immigrants value family above all else and may rely less on text and more on context for meaning.
- *Product displays:* The way you display products can often attract or turn away prospective customers. Consult with someone from the culture you're trying to attract to assist you in creating appropriate product displays.
- *Signage:* If you have a store or business that your clients will visit, make sure any signs you have (including signs in the parking lot) are understandable to your target clientele.

- *Product selection:* All the marketing and advertising in the world will do you no good unless you offer the products and services that your multicultural clientele want to buy. Have your front-line staff ask customers whether they can help them find any-thing, and keep a careful record of what customers want—then, make sure you have it in stock and on display.

- *Sales:* Every salesperson should obtain training in, or at least a book on, cross-cultural sales.

- *Customer service:* Anyone who deals directly with customers, including your receptionist, should obtain training to establish at least a base level of cultural competency. Insensitivity to a customer's cultural differences and needs after the sale can harm repeat and referral business.

- *Hours of operation:* New immigrants are likely to work longer hours than most of your traditional clientele. Make sure your days and hours of operation are convenient for the clients you are trying to attract.

- *Location:* If you already have an established business, changing its location to appeal to a different group of clients may not be realistic, but if possible, choose a convenient, safe location for your business that has plenty of parking.

Lee recommends that you consult with customers and other busi-ness owners in the community to discuss ideas on how to more effectively serve your clientele. Consider assembling an advisory board with at least one member from the culture you're trying to cater to and perhaps some community leaders. Ask them to au-dit your business and marketing efforts to identify areas that need improvement.

Ralph's Rule: Give your business a multicultural makeover. Advertising and selling to customers from other cultures is not enough. You need to make sure you're offering the products and services that appeal to your customers and that you treat all customers the way they want to be treated before, during, and after the sale.

AVOID OR RECOVER FROM A SALES SLUMP

More than 50 million Americans are now in sales, either in home-based businesses or in a career selling cars or trucks, real estate, mortgages, clothing, you name it. And of those 50 million salespeople, probably 40 million of them, or 80 percent of the entire field, at any one time are in a sales slump. A slump can last an hour, a day, a week, a month, or even longer. These slumps may be inevitable, but if you want to stay in sales as a career, you cannot sit back and wait for better days to come. You've got to take deliberate steps to break out.

Some of the following steps have helped me and others I have coached and trained emerge from a sales slump.

AVOID NEGATIVE PEOPLE AND SITUATIONS

There is nothing worse than talking about negative situations in the workplace. Avoid the water cooler or coffee room where people moan all day about how terrible things are. To break out of the slump, you need all your positive energy. Talking about bad stuff will only bring you down just when you need to feel great. For more about the power of a positive attitude, look back at Week 4.

SET A START DATE

Break your sales slide by getting back to the basics. You may want to increase the number of new daily contacts you make from 25 to 50 or even 100. There's nothing like taking decisive action for breaking out of a slow period. Weeks 22 to 24 present some strategies for increasing your number of daily contacts.

BE COMMITTED

Breaking the sales slump is not easy, but it can be done. Continue to be committed. Once you recognize that you are in a sales slump, you can begin to initiate change. You also realize you have had these setbacks before and will probably have them again.

MAKE MARKETING A REGULAR ACTIVITY

If you make marketing a routine activity, something you do in good times and bad, you'll find that your slumps come less frequently and don't last as long. It's the salespeople who ignore marketing when times are good and do it only when times are bad who find their sales valleys deeper and longer.

KEEP RECORDS

I encourage you to get involved in some day planning system. Prior to using a computer for *everything,* I relied heavily on my Franklin Day Planner. Google has a great free online calendar, which you can learn about by visiting www.google.com/calendar. You can even share calendars with friends, family members, and colleagues to help coordinate your schedules. If you have Microsoft Office, you can use Outlook's Calendar to manage your schedule.

To be successful, you must be able to go back and look at a certain week, certain day, certain time frame, and say why your units or sales weren't what you wanted them to be. Perhaps you weren't marketing your prospecting calls the week before or perhaps you spent too much time on paperwork and not enough meeting customers. Records will tell you that.

TALK TO YOUR MANAGER ABOUT
YOUR SALES DECLINE

If management doesn't bring it up, approach your manager. Chances are your manager has experienced similar slumps before and has some idea about what's wrong. At the very least, talking through the problem may relieve the feeling of isolation that comes with a slump.

LEARN FROM PAST MISTAKES

Think about what helped you in the past. Think about what hurt you in the past. A common myth is that successful people make few, if any, mistakes. This is rarely true. In fact, successful people tend to make more mistakes than others, because they take more risks. However, they usually avoid making the same mistake twice.

After every major undertaking, do a postmortem to evaluate what worked and what didn't. Do more of what works and less of what doesn't, so your investments of time, energy, and resources will have a more positive effect.

GET YOUR FAMILY AND FRIENDS INVOLVED

Make it a contest. For example, tell your friends or family that if you're the top salesperson of the month, the following month you'll take them to a theme park for a long weekend. If you're the top salesperson of the week, the family gets to go out to dinner. Getting your family excited about your success will motivate them to motivate you with their support and suggestions.

LEARN TO COPE

You have to learn that sales slumps happen to everyone, even the top producers. You will get out of them. They will happen again. I can feel a sales slump coming long before anyone else notices. When I sense a slump, sometimes in the middle of the day, I get up from my desk, walk around the office, and tell myself that I just have to make things happen.

Ralph's Rule: Slumps are inevitable, but they don't have to come as often or last as long as you think they might.

BUILD YOUR OWN SALES TEAM

D uring Week 8, I encouraged you to hire an assistant to attend to any and all delegate-able tasks, including answering phones, completing sales reports, processing transactions, and managing your schedule. Now that you are in Week 47 of your sales training, I think you are ready to take your sales career to the next level, and there is no better way to do this than by building your own sales team.

WHAT IS A SALES TEAM?

By definition, a team is a group of people working together for a common purpose, but it's really much more than that. A team is an entity with diverse skills, talents, and personalities. It is a whole that is greater than the sum of its parts, enabling each individual to accomplish more than they would otherwise be able to do by themselves. A team's diversity makes it more capable of meeting challenges, and its flexibility enables the team to quickly adapt to changing conditions.

Although every sales team is unique, most start out as a fairly simple two-person team—the salesperson and his or her assistant. The salesperson does what he or she is best at and performs the most dollar-productive activities—activities that drive business and generate revenue. The assistant fills a supporting role—scheduling, processing paperwork, and performing other tasks to free up the salesperson's time and resources to focus on even more dollar-productive activities.

When salespeople realize how much more productive and profitable they are with an assistant, they usually decide to grow their team. Sales teams can become small-businesses unto themselves. The team can vary in size and structure, with some complex teams having numerous team members who play the following roles (sometimes one person can play more than one role):

- *Rainmaker and team leader:* Usually the most experienced and energetic salesperson—the one who puts a face on the team, promotes it, networks, builds relationships, and generates the most business.
- *Team manager (second in command):* The person who keeps the team on track, oversees operations, double-checks the accounting, and runs the meetings.
- *Transaction manager:* The transaction manager processes transactions from the point of sale to the closing.
- *Client care (customer service representative):* The front-line team member who meets and greets clients, addresses most of their needs, answers most of their questions, and refers clients to others when he or she does not know the answer.
- *Assistants:* One or more people to manage daily activities, such as assembling marketing packets, updating Web sites and blogs, performing market research, fielding general questions from clients, and so on.
- *Professional office organizer:* The office organizer makes sure everything has a place and everything is in its place. Although this may seem like a fairly mundane job, far too many teams waste time looking for misplaced documents and supplies.
- *Courier (delivery person):* The courier is basically in charge of running the team's shipping department, making sure all packages reach their destination. That can mean dropping off packages at the post office or delivering them in person.
- *Public relations/marketing manager:* The public relations (PR) person or marketing manager is in charge of marketing the team

and generating positive press through as many media outlets as possible, including the Web, e-mail, TV, radio, print (advertising and articles), podcasts, and videocasts. This person may also function as the team blogger or ghost blogger.

- *IT (information technology) specialist:* This person keeps the computers running and may also create and manage the team's Web sites and blogs.

REALIZE THE BENEFITS OF THE TEAM-BASED APPROACH

Salespeople who successfully make the transition to a team-based system rarely regret their decision. What they regret is not having done it sooner. They often tell me about how frustrated and overworked they were prior to building a team. Working over 80 hours a week, having insufficient time and resources for their clients, salespeople often find themselves making costly mistakes and having little time for themselves and their families.

After establishing a team, their lives quickly improved. These salespeople were able to focus on what they did best—dealing with clients and selling product—and could outsource the rest to other team members who had the time, resources, and energy to take on those tasks. Yes, they had to share their profits with the rest of the team, but the increase in commissions was more than enough to cover the added expense. Perhaps best of all, these salespeople had more time and energy for themselves and their family, friends, and communities.

Team-based salespeople are overwhelmingly more satisfied with their careers and with their lives in general than are salespeople who work alone, primarily due to the following benefits of team-based selling:

- *Increased personal productivity:* When someone else is handling what you feel are mundane tasks and distractions, you can do more of what you love to do more efficiently.
- *Increased office efficiency:* Division of labor always increases efficiency by delegating tasks to team members who specialize in performing those tasks.
- *Increased sales and profits:* With your focus solely on networking and selling, sales and profits will soar.

- *More and better opportunities:* More people means more skills and talents, which translates into opportunities. Inventory your team's skills and try to identify new business opportunities that can tap your team's potential.

- *Improved customer service:* Other team members can handle minor issues, so you can deal with any higher-end issues that arise, providing superior service to all of your customers.

- *More free time:* In addition to having more free time on a daily basis, you can now feel more comfortable taking some weekends off and going on vacation, knowing that you have people to cover for you.

ARE YOU TEAM-READY?

I believe so strongly in the team-based approach to selling that I recommend it to every salesperson I meet, mentor, coach, or train. I believe that it not only boosts revenue and profits, but also helps overworked salespeople establish a balance between their personal and professional lives. It makes for happier individuals and healthier families and communities.

However, not everyone is cut out to be a team player or has a sufficient amount of business to justify forming a sales team. Forming a team prematurely can result in catastrophe, so before you begin, make sure your situation meets the following criteria:

- You have more business than you can handle on your own or are convinced that creating a team will bring in more business than you can handle on your own.

- You have at least two months worth of reserves to cover the cost of adding team members.

- You have sufficient revenue coming in to pay new team members' commissions or salaries.

- You can delegate tasks and pass responsibilities to others. If you are a control freak, you may still be able to implement a team-based approach, but you will probably need to hire a manager who is better suited to delegating tasks.

- You have procedures in place to train new team members, as discussed in Week 7.

- You have office space and equipment that new team members will need or it is realistic to expect other team members to bring whatever they need to do their jobs.

TAKE A LESSON FROM YOUR DENTIST

Most dentists don't work as their own receptionists or clean patients' teeth. They hire a receptionist to answer phones, greet patients, process insurance information, and bill patients. They hire dental hygienists to clean teeth, take x-rays, and prepare patients for their dental exams.

If your dentist runs an efficient office, he or she probably spends about 5 or 10 minutes with you for your six-month checkup, primarily to find out how you're doing and quickly examine the inside of your mouth for any potential problems. Your dentist offloads all the lower-level tasks and then focuses on higher-level tasks, such as fixing cavities, capping teeth, and referring patients to specialists.

To maximize your own efficiency as a salesperson, take a lesson from your dentist and learn to streamline procedures. Apply the assembly-line approach to selling, as discussed in Week 7, and assemble a team to handle the sale from start to finish. While you focus on selling and on serving your customers, the rest of your team can handle all the details that keep your office running.

Ralph's Rule: Start small, with one assistant, as discussed in Week 8, and then start growing your team by adding people with the right personalities, work ethics, skills, and talents. Train them well, and then give them the real responsibility to make decisions.

WEEK 48

SHARPEN YOUR TEAM MANAGEMENT SKILLS

About 18 years ago, I decided to open my own sales company. Before that, I had always worked for others. During my earlier years, I had had personal assistants working for me. But it was only when I opened my own company that I became a sales manager as well as doing my own sales.

At first, I made all the same dumb mistakes that most sales managers make. For example, I alienated my support staff. I didn't realize how left out they felt when I set up contests for our salespeople and would reward top producers with prizes and bonuses. I lost some good people. Today, I try to bring in the support people by getting them involved in the success of the company and rewarding them accordingly. They contribute through sales leads, suggestions, and the like. It's really made a difference—in the numbers, yes, but more so in the general office environment.

Another mistake I made: I assumed that everyone was motivated primarily by money. I found that if you rely primarily on cash and commissions to motivate your salespeople, you'll probably have short-term success, but you tend to lose your top people to your competition and suffer high turnover in general. Salespeople crave recognition—it's all about ego for them. Bringing in $1 million is great, but the good ones care more about how they compare to their peers than how much they brought in. If they aren't recognized as part of an elite group, the dollar amount doesn't mean much—it has no value outside of the commission for them. If you want to turn salespeople into order takers, use a commission system as your sole reward system.

The best thing you can do is to ask them how they want to be rewarded. Don't just promote them to sales managers. This is usually a waste of a good salesperson. In terms of ego, they will initially be pleased with the promotion and the increased power and responsibility, but the promotion takes them away from their strength—selling.

Ask a top person how he or she prefers to be rewarded. Maybe the person wants to branch out to a different line of sales or wants to personalize his or her own reward system. One of my best people left me when I didn't understand that he wanted to sell fewer homes at higher prices, instead of my way—selling more homes at lower prices. Actually our systems would have produced about the same revenue, but his was more efficient. When he saw my goals for him (selling substantially more houses), he quit. He felt I had no idea what motivated him and what success meant to him. I goofed up. I didn't listen to him and what he wanted.

Sometimes you can reward people by giving them better tools to do their jobs. My secretary once asked me for her own fax machine next to her desk so she wouldn't have to stand in line down the hall to fax a document. One of my buyer agents asked me for his own computer for his desk so he wouldn't have to share one. These are both top people and giving them these things was a no-brainer. It made them happier and even more productive.

To motivate people now, I do weekend getaways and contests. I put a lot of energy into recognition, including little things like thank-you notes. Also, I try to pull my people out of their sales cocoons. Part of being a good sales team is being creative and thinking outside your immediate surroundings. For example, when I go to sporting events, I always ask myself how I could get $10 from every person there. Some of my schemes are fairly ridiculous, but that isn't the point. It's a great game I play with myself to help keep my creative juices flowing.

Another big mistake that sales managers often make is they forget to manage and revert back to their sales behavior. You see this with people who have been promoted to manager when they never should have been or they simply haven't gotten the training they so desperately need.

This can happen when the salesperson brings them along to help seal a deal. In general, I think it's a great idea to bring along a sales manager in the final negotiations. It makes the client feel important, and the manager is supposed to make the salesperson look good in front of the client. I recommend it 100 percent. But it can backfire when the manager wants to hog the spotlight. The manager is so excited to be back in the middle of a sale that his ego wants all the attention. So he pushes the salesperson into the background.

How can the salesperson develop a relationship with the client when the client sees that salesperson as a second-string player? The manager is sabotaging his salesperson. He must remember the manager's job is to help his people achieve their goals. He has to change the way he thinks about success. It is no longer based on his own numbers, but on how good his team's numbers are. Taking this step back is tough for successful salespeople because they are so used to being hands-on.

I've made all these mistakes and more but I try to learn from them. I'm a better manager and motivator now than I was 18 years ago, and I hope to be even better tomorrow. You can be, too!

Ralph's Rule: The key to good sales management is to realize that managing is different from selling. It requires different skills and a different view of what's important. Don't try managing unless you're willing to understand this difference.

CLOSE A SALE THE RIGHT WAY: SIX FOLLOW-UP STEPS

W e all lose deals. I hate it. Sometimes we lose when the customer says "No," and sometimes we lose after a contract is already signed but the deal falls apart. I work so hard to make sales happen that I just *hate* it when I lose one. Still, it happens, so we have to be prepared. Here's my checklist of things to do near the end of a closing that starts to go south or eventually slips through your fingers.

1. SAVE IT!

If you feel that a deal is slipping through your fingers, try to salvage it—somehow. You'd be surprised at how many salespeople just give up on a deal when they encounter a few snags. They'll consider it lost and move on to the next one. Not me. I believe that 75 percent of "lost" sales can be saved. It takes more work, but a deal saved is a sale made.

Let me give you an example. I was showing a home for sale, and the buyers made an offer contingent upon an inspection. This is standard practice. Well, the inspector found a few inches of standing water in the crawl space in the basement. The buyers wanted to pull out of the deal. But I really wanted to save this sale, so I dug into the situation. I learned from the inspector that the sump pump was defective. The pump wasn't doing its job, and that's why the water had begun to collect. It would cost $250 to fix the pump. I got the seller to pay for the new pump and then I brought my buyers back for another look. They were satisfied that the problem had been fixed. Result: Another sale!

Many potentially "lost" deals can be saved in this way. Never give up on a deal until you've done everything in your power to save it.

2. WHEN YOU LOSE A SALE, FIND OUT WHY

Okay, so you've hit one of those walls where you just cannot get the sale you've worked on for so long. When this happens, I make a practice of asking the customers why they chose to go in another direction. (Mind you now, I'm not talking about casual shoppers—I'm talking about losing customers who were qualified and ready to buy.) Often, they'll tell me up front. They'll say I was too aggressive, or that they promised a family member they'd use another salesperson, or some other reason. And I always say, "Thanks, that's helpful information, we're always trying to improve."

There are two reasons that I bother to ask. First, the information often is helpful. If I'm coming across as too aggressive too often, maybe I'll tone down my presentation. We all need feedback, and what better feedback than from our customers? But, second, I also use the information to know how to approach those same customers the next time. If, for example, they used another salesperson only because a family member suggested it, that sale has a good chance of not working out because the customers are choosing a salesperson for the wrong reason. That's good to know when I approach them again.

3. STAY IN TOUCH WITH THEM

A lot of customers who go elsewhere come to regret it. Maybe the other salesperson your customer chose over-promised and under-delivered. Quite often, I've found that a customer who gives me an emphatic no is ready to do business with me a month later.

Let me tell you about my friend Jonathan Dwoskin. Jonathan was a top account executive with U.S. Web, one of the largest and best of the Internet consulting firms. I knew the quality of their work because the company was the first to design my web site at RalphRoberts.com. At the time, Jonathan was chasing a deal with a major customer who eventually went with another web designer. The customer had wanted to hire a firm that could handle its public relations (PR) as well as its Internet site. Jonathan said U.S. Web would be happy to bring in a good PR firm as part of its package, but didn't keep that function in-house because U.S. Web wants to focus only on what it does best. Well, the customer went with another Web consultant that promised everything.

"After I lost it, I called her every month," Jonathan says of this customer. "I would ask, 'Are things going okay? Are you being treated like you want?' I continually built that relationship." He never gave up, but always let the customer know in a quiet, professional way that U.S. Web stood ready to serve it.

Well, just before the customer's web site was to debut—and it was the focus of a huge nationwide marketing campaign that had already been printed—the customer called Jonathan in a panic. The first provider had been unable to deliver. The customer was 10 days shy of launching the campaign and had to meet deadline. Could Jonathan's team take over and finish on time?

Well, they did. Jonathan estimates that this one customer resulted in about a half-million dollars' worth of business over time. U.S. Web got the deal in the end probably for a lot of reasons and not only because Jonathan stayed in touch after he "lost" the first sale. But surely it helped that Jonathan was smart enough to know that a deal isn't lost until your competitor has delivered the goods.

4. THANK THEM FOR THEIR TIME

This is simple courtesy, and it's always good business. You can thank them verbally, send them a note, or even send them flowers or a gift. Consider it part of your marketing budget. It will certainly impress those potential customers with your desire to have them as clients.

5. ASK FOR A REFERRAL

A lot of customers may be impressed with your knowledge and professionalism even if they don't sign a contract. They may be willing to refer others to you even though they themselves choose someone else. Ask!

6. MOVE ON

When you really lose a sale, don't dwell on the failure. Move on! You're a professional, and you know that losses are just part of the game. Your next sale may be just around the corner.

Ralph's Rule: Failure is part of our business, so you'll need a game plan for dealing with it. Once you have your plan in place, review it frequently. You'll find that losing a deal isn't the terrible setback you once thought it was.

BECOME A LIFELONG LEARNER

You are only as good as the people you meet, the books you read, and the tapes you listen to.

—Charlie "Tremendous" Jones

The pace of change both in the world and almost certainly in your industry is rapidly accelerating. Technology is streamlining operations, transforming markets into global communities, and enabling salespeople to go mobile. You can now vacation on the French Riviera while following up with clients in Colorado. In addition, selling is becoming more of a team sport, empowering sales teams to increase efficiency and boost both productivity and profits.

To thrive in this world of ever-increasing change, you have to keep up with the latest information and technology. You must constantly educate yourself in order to adapt and take advantage of new tools and opportunities that change delivers to your doorstep. You must become a lifelong learner.

Yet, when I talk to salespeople, I hear all too frequently that they just "don't have the time to keep up." I know real estate agents who subscribe to RISMedia's *Power Team Report* and *Power Broker Networking Report* and don't even take the time to read these valuable publications—publications that could ultimately save them tons more time than is required to read the articles.

Tip: Remember, the more you know, the more you need to know. And, when the student is ready, the teacher appears.

Some salespeople refuse to attend industry conferences, falsely assuming that they are a big waste of time and resources. Many salespeople won't even crack open a book to learn a new sales or marketing technique or listen to an audio book. All of these salespeople are losing out big-time—in time, profits, and personal fulfillment.

Becoming a lifelong learner means plugging yourself into the industry grapevine. Here are some suggestions on how to do just that:

- Attend at least one industry conference every year. You can usually find one or two valuable sessions or speakers, and even if you don't, the networking opportunities alone make the investment well worth it. In Week 42, I discussed the importance of attending conferences and seminars.

- Read several articles a day on industry-related topics that interest you. Go to Google News (news.google.com), click "News Alerts" in the left navigation bar, and set up news alerts to have Google automatically notify you about late-breaking news on topics of interest. (Enter very specific search instructions, so you are not inundated with irrelevant articles.) You need to know what's happening in your industry as well as in your market. I spend about an hour every morning checking and reading my Google News Alerts stories.

- Pick up a book about selling or any business-related topic that interests you and start reading. You can find plenty of great books on the market that reveal new techniques you may never have discovered on your own and can teach you new skills. In addition, reading always stimulates thinking and inspires you to come up with your own innovative ideas.

- Listen to tapes, CDs, or podcasts from the top salespeople and motivational speakers. If you usually listen to music as you're driving to meet clients, consider listening to something that's a little more educational.

- Take classes and obtain certifications. Taking a class can help motivate you and hold you accountable for learning the information. You can take classes on sales techniques, management, customer service, cross-cultural selling, or industry-specific topics. Get certified in a particular area and you obtain instant credibility.

- Learn new technologies. Spend time learning how to make optimum use of your computer and the software installed on it. Explore your software's help systems, read a book, or take a class to learn how to boost productivity with features you may not even be aware of. Focus your efforts on learning more about Internet marketing through web sites and blogs. In Week 26, I encourage you to learn new technologies.

- Connect with a mentor or coach. One of the best ways to learn fast is to connect with a top producer. Consider shadowing a real estate professional whom you admire or asking the person to act as your mentor or coach. Success leaves big footprints. Follow them. Skip back to Week 32 to learn more about pursuing opportunities to shadow top producers.

- Subscribe to online newsletters related to your industry or to other topics you would like to explore.

- Get an iPod and take advantage of books on tape, podcasts, and other electronic media.

- Become involved in a community group that can provide you with contacts and knowledge.

- Take a class at your local community college or community adult education center that is totally out of your realm—believe it or not, you will find something there that you can transfer to your industry.

- Partner with someone who is willing to exchange knowledge.

You do not need to limit your studies to topics related to your industry and the sales profession. Recently at a surprise birthday party for my nephew, someone I have known for some time, a retired GM executive, told me of his recent interest in genealogy (the second most popular subject on the Internet). He is having a great time with it, researching his own family tree and learning about world history and geography at the same time.

I know, I am probably preaching to the choir. The fact that you are reading this is proof that you are part of the minority of salespeople who actually care enough about your profession to become a student of it. Others in our field, perhaps even some of your closest colleagues haven't gotten the memo. Do them a favor. Send them a copy of this book. Working together, we might just be able to convince our colleagues to take at least one step toward improving their future.

Ralph's Rule: People who think they know everything are often the most ignorant and arrogant of the bunch. No matter how successful you are, there's always room for improvement. Be curious and keep on learning to become a better salesperson and a better person overall.

WEEK 51

JUST DO IT!

O ne of my acquaintances, Pat Donofrio, served as Macomb County circuit court judge until about 2002 at which time he was appointed to the Michigan court of appeals. In 2004, he was elected to a six-year term. No matter what opinion you hold about lawyers, salespeople could learn a lot from this particular judge about good work habits. I know I have. And I'd like to share Pat's story with you.

When he became a judge in early 1997, his circuit had a five-year backlog of civil litigation. Pat believes in the old saying that justice delayed is justice denied. He made it his business to stay at work until he had accomplished everything to stay current.

This meant holding court at night and on weekends. It also meant turning around the policy of granting unlimited delays in lawsuits. Instead, Pat would call the parties into his chambers, address the issues in dispute, and keep the parties talking to each other until they agreed on a settlement.

"My view is the clock doesn't have enough hours in it," Pat told me. "The way to lead is by example and that translates into hard work. I used to run my law firm the same way. If you want subordinates to work hard, you have to show them that work is valued and that you work hard yourself."

In most of this book, I've been teaching you ways to work smarter. But sometimes, salespeople have to follow Judge Donofrio's example and work harder as well as smarter. As Nike says, "Just do it!"

The rewards will come. For salespeople, working harder usually means making more money. In many ways, sales remain a numbers game. Up to a point, the more people you contact, the more sales you'll have.

I say "up to a point" because there are limits to hard work. When I was a younger man, I routinely worked 100-hour weeks. My goal was to be home before the end of *Nightline*, which aired at about 11:30 PM in Detroit. I was obsessed with my job for years. The result is that I almost killed myself with a poor diet, too much work, and never seeing my family.

In recent years, I've managed to tame this obsession. Now I have what I describe as a "healthy obsession." I work probably 50 hours a week and schedule regular time off for my family and friends.

If you're in sales and you're working 40 hours a week, you're leaving money behind on the table. No one can work 40 hours a week and make all the sales calls and handle the paperwork and do networking and self-promotion. You may be able to get away with working 40 hours a week occasionally, but other times you'll have to put in longer hours to achieve the level of success you desire.

Working harder is especially important when you face a major backlog, as Pat Donofrio did. "The best way is to roll up your sleeves and get to work," he says.

By the way, Pat found that working harder also had a positive effect on the lawyers and parties to lawsuits. When they found out that he intended to keep them there until they settled, or to go to trial in the near future, it concentrated their minds on the problem, which led to quicker, and better, decision making. The whole process got more efficient. Remember how the O. J. Simpson trial lasted more than a year? Pat completed 38 trials in 54 weeks.

Just as you should involve your customers and employees in your hard work, Pat has always tried to get the parties involved in a suit to really understand what was behind his efforts. "I want them to buy into the process of reaching a resolution. I think it's important that litigants feel part of the process, not that it's just two lawyers talking to the judge in his chamber."

In one case, for example, two lawyers came in, each seeking a restraining order against the other's client. It was a typical business dispute. Many judges would have routinely granted one or the other order or both. But, Pat says, "I don't just sign orders." Instead, he called the clients into his chambers and spent two hours exploring the case. By the end of that time, the parties were ready to put a settlement agreement on the record.

"The sooner you get to the central issues, the sooner you can get to a resolution," Pat says.

What I hope you take away from this chapter is a commitment to clearing away your own backlogs. And to keep you focused on that goal, here are some tips for working smarter while you work harder.

PLAN

Nothing focuses you on the essential tasks as well as daily and weekly planning. Each morning I take 15 minutes and type up a list of things to do and what I want to accomplish that day. I put in personal as well as business goals. Once I list all the tasks, I prioritize them so I know what to do first. I then e-mail my list to Lois, my second in command, and/or to other assistants who can help me accomplish everything. This is my way, as Pat says, to get to the central issues.

Without planning, you'll bounce from crisis to crisis with no idea what you should be doing next. Without planning, you'll be working longer hours and getting less done. I predict that if you work the same number of hours you do now, but add 15 minutes of daily planning, you'll see an increase in your sales and profits.

For more about planning, review Week 6.

DELEGATE

One of my keys to success has been learning to delegate. In his courtroom, Pat has someone to assist him, and of course there are many employees in the court clerk's office to keep track of the voluminous files. In the same way, I've always had assistants, right from the very beginning. When I was a 19-year-old novice just entering sales, I hired a teenage co-op student to answer the phones for me after school. I had my own secretary and several personal assistants handling paperwork for me long before it was fashionable in the real estate industry. In fact, one of the reasons that more real estate agents have assistants is that I popularized the idea in the 1980s and early 1990s.

Delegation frees you to spend your time on the really important matters—meeting with customers, networking, and strategic planning for the future.

Start with one assistant, as I encourage you to do during Week 8. When you are more comfortable delegating tasks and are generating sufficient sales and revenue to afford more assistants, consider building your own sales team, as I discuss in Week 47.

USE TECHNOLOGY TO LEVERAGE YOUR EFFORTS

Today's court system couldn't run without computers. In the same way, I've always invested in new technology to gain an edge. I use everything from a satellite route-finding system in my SUV to more traditional things like telephones and fax machines. Each type of technology either multiplies my efforts or enables me to concentrate more on what's most important.

For example, my satellite navigation system frees me from worrying over directions. I just type in the destination, and the system directs me, right down to telling me where to turn and when. I have always found that technology buys me free hours to devote to actual selling. Some new piece of technology may cost a lot, but the new transactions I do more than pay for my investment.

To learn more about putting the latest technologies to work for you, review Week 26.

KNOW WHEN TO TAKE A BREAK

There comes a time when every salesperson hits the wall of exhaustion. Whether it happens to you at 60 hours a week or 100 hours a week, learn to recognize the symptoms. If your family complains about never seeing you, if problems in the office leave you edgy all the time, if your production seems to be leveling off or even falling no matter how hard you work, it's time to take some time off. You'll come back feeling refreshed and ready to work again.

But don't use your need for a break to justify slacking off when you should be selling. I think more sales are lost around the water cooler and the coffee machine than just about anywhere else. Patricia Tripp, a British hairdresser who became an internationally famous motivational speaker, says she used to view lunch hour as a time to squeeze in three more appointments. That's my advice, too.

Work smarter, yes, but work harder, too.

Case closed.

Ralph's Rule: Don't go into sales if you don't want to work hard. There may be limits to this approach, but generally the harder you work, the more money you earn.

WEEK 52

FINAL THOUGHTS

We just have time for a few more bits of wisdom I have discovered during the course of my 30-year career in sales. If I had to distill everything I've learned, it would go like this:

- Don't concentrate on making a lot of money. Concentrate on being the kind of person with whom other people want to do business.
- Renew yourself at regular intervals with time off for family, friends, and hobbies.
- God gave you two ears and one mouth. If you use them in that proportion, you'll come out all right.
- Embrace change, don't fear it or resist it. In every change lies the promise of new opportunity.
- People have to know that you care before they care about what you know.
- Don't settle for anything less than doing things just a little bit better than anybody else.
- Take risks. People tend to regret more of what they didn't do than mistakes they've made.
- Good planning remains the essence of time management.
- A dishonest presentation is bad for your customer and will ruin your reputation.

- Never badmouth the competition. It just cheapens you in the eyes of your customers.
- Lunch hours are for talking to customers you can't reach during normal business hours.
- Remember the 80/20 rule. Eighty percent of your business comes from 20 percent of your clients.
- Learn to delegate. If you don't have an assistant, you are one.
- Maybe half your client base will change their jobs, their houses, or their financial circumstances within a year's time, so your marketing efforts have to be updated frequently.
- Put your photograph on all your marketing materials. People can't buy from you if they don't know who you are.
- Even after you're established, spend at least 5 percent of your budget on marketing and self-promotion.
- Your most recent customer can be your hottest prospect for your next sale.
- Most of my customers have bought or sold a home at least once before they met me. That means that some other salesperson didn't nurture that relationship enough to retain them. Don't let that salesperson be you.
- Don't prejudge anybody. A waitress or a car valet may have a wider circle of acquaintances than anyone else you know.
- Always remember to thank people. Thank them in person, thank them in writing, and don't forget to stay in touch.
- A past customer or a referral should always take precedence over an entirely new customer.
- If you don't ask, the answer is always no.
- "No" means "know"—your customer doesn't yet *know* enough to say "yes."

Ralph's Rule: A book like this can help boost your productivity only if you put what you've learned into practice.

About the Authors

Ralph R. Roberts' sales success is legendary. He has been profiled by the Associated Press, CNN, and *Time* magazine, and was once dubbed by *Time* magazine "the best selling Realtor in America." In addition to being one of the most successful salespeople in America, Ralph is also an experienced mentor, coach, consultant, and author. He has written and co-authored several successful books, including *Advanced Selling For Dummies, Cross-Cultural Selling For Dummies, Walk Like a Giant, Sell Like a Madman, Mortgage Myths: 77 Secrets That Will Save You Thousands on Home Financing,* and *Foreclosure Investing For Dummies* (John Wiley & Sons), *Real Wealth by Investing in Real Estate* (Prentice Hall), and *Protect Yourself from Real Estate and Mortgage Fraud* (Kaplan).

Although Ralph has many varied skills and interests, his true passion is selling and showing other salespeople how to boost their sales and profits. In *52 Weeks of Sales Success,* Ralph reveals the practical sales tips and tricks he's gathered over the course of his more than 30-year career and challenges you to put them to work for yourself. To find out more about Ralph Roberts, visit www.AboutRalph .com.

Joe Kraynak is a freelance author who has written and co-authored dozens of books on topics ranging from slam poetry to computer basics. Joe began his career writing beginner-level computer books solo. He now teams up with experts in various fields to co-author and promote books on topics that he finds fascinating. In *52 Weeks of Sales Success*, Joe and Ralph join forces to deliver an everything-you-need-to-know-about-selling course in 52 weeks. To find out more about Joe, visit his blog at joekraynak.com.

Index